ARTHUR ASHE

ARTHUR ASHE

Ted Weissberg

Senior Consulting Editor
Nathan Irvin Huggins
Director
W.E.B. Du Bois Institute for Afro-American Research
Harvard University

GROLIER INCORPORATED
Danbury, Connecticut

Chelsea House Publishers
Editor-in-Chief Remmel Nunn
Managing Editor Karyn Gullen Browne
Copy Chief Juliann Barbato
Picture Editor Adrian G. Allen
Art Director Maria Epes
Deputy Copy Chief Mark Rifkin
Assistant Art Director Noreen Romano
Manufacturing Manager Gerald Levine
Systems Manager Lindsey Ottman
Production Manager Joseph Romano
Production Coordinator Marie Claire Cebrián

Black Americans of Achievement
Senior Editor Richard Rennert

Staff for ARTHUR ASHE
Editorial Assistant Michele Haddad
Picture Researcher Diana Gongora
Designer Ghila Krajzman
Cover Illustration Daniel Mark Duffy

UPDATED TO 1992

5 7 9 8 6 4

Library of Congress Cataloging-in-Publication Data

Weissberg, Ted.
    Arthur Ashe—tennis great/by Ted Weissberg.
        p.   cm.
    Includes bibliographical references and index.
    Summary: Presents the life of an important black athlete and
tennis player, Arthur Ashe.
    ISBN 0-7910-1115-1
        0-7910-1141-0 (pbk.)
    1. Ashe, Arthur—Juvenile literature.   2. Tennis players—
United States—Biography—Juvenile literature.
    [1. Ashe, Arthur.   2. Tennis players.   3. Afro-Americans—
Biography.]
    I. Title.
GV994.A7W45   1991
92—dc20   90-43040
[796.342′092]   CIP
[B]   AC

Published for Grolier by Chelsea House

Frontispiece: *Arthur Ashe displays the winning form that earned him the title of America's top-ranked amateur at age 25.*

CONTENTS

———⬥———

ON
ACHIEVEMENT

———— •❦• ————

Coretta Scott King

BEFORE YOU BEGIN this book, I hope you will ask yourself what the word excellence means to you. I think that it's a question we should all ask, and keep asking as we grow older and change. Because the truest answer to it should never change. When you think of excellence, perhaps you think of success at work; or of becoming wealthy; or meeting the right person, getting married, and having a good family life.

Those important goals are worth striving for, but there is a better way to look at excellence. As Martin Luther King, Jr., said in one of his last sermons, "I want you to be first in love. I want you to be first in moral excellence. I want you to be first in generosity. If you want to be important, wonderful. If you want to be great, wonderful. But recognize that he who is greatest among you shall be your servant."

My husband, Martin Luther King, Jr., knew that the true meaning of achievement is service. When I met him, in 1952, he was already ordained as a Baptist preacher and was working towards a doctoral degree at Boston University. I was studying at the New England Conservatory and dreamed of accomplishments in music. We married a year later, and after I graduated the following year we moved to Montgomery, Alabama. We didn't know it then, but our notions of achievement were about to undergo a dramatic change.

You may have read or heard about what happened next. What began with the boycott of a local bus line grew into a national movement, and by the time he was assassinated in 1968 my husband had fashioned a black movement powerful enough to shatter forever the practice of racial segregation. What you may not have read about is where he got his method for resisting injustice without compromising his religious beliefs.

He adopted the strategy of nonviolence from a man of a different race, who lived in a distant country, and even practiced a different religion. The man was Mahatma Gandhi, the great leader of India, who devoted his life to serving humanity in the spirit of love and nonviolence. It was in these principles that Martin discovered his method for social reform. More than anything else, those two principles were the key to his achievements.

This book is about black Americans who served society through the excellence of their achievements. It forms a part of the rich history of black men and women in America—a history of stunning accomplishments in every field of human endeavor, from literature and art to science, industry, education, diplomacy, athletics, jurisprudence, even polar exploration.

Not all of the people in this history had the same ideals, but I think you will find something that all of them have in common. Like Martin Luther King, Jr., they all decided to become "drum majors" and serve humanity. In that principle—whether it was expressed in books, inventions, or song—they found something outside themselves to use as a goal and a guide. Something that showed them a way to serve others, instead of living only for themselves.

Reading the stories of these courageous men and women not only helps us discover the principles that we will use to guide our own lives but also teaches us about our black heritage and about America itself. It is crucial for us to know the heroes and heroines of our history and to realize that the price we paid in our struggle for equality in America was dear. But we must also understand that we have gotten as far as we have partly because America's democratic system and ideals made it possible.

We are still struggling with racism and prejudice. But the great men and women in this series are a tribute to the spirit of our democratic ideals and the system in which they have flourished. And that makes their stories special and worth knowing. ❦

ARTHUR
ASHE

1

A MASTERSTROKE
AT WIMBLEDON

T HE ALL-ENGLAND LAWN Tennis and Croquet Club, located in the London suburb of Wimbledon, has been the mecca of the tennis world for
more than a century. The first tournament in lawn-
tennis history was held there in 1877, just 4 years
after Major Walter Clopton Wingfield invented the
sport in Wales, adapting it from the 700-year-old
game of court tennis. Since then, every one of the
sport's greatest stars has, at one time or another,
played in the club's annual All-England Championships, also known as Wimbledon.

The sport's oldest and most celebrated tournament is its most tradition-bound event as well. All
of the matches are held on grass courts, as they were
in Major Wingfield's day, and every player is required
to wear a predominantly white outfit. (The top-
ranked players are given the privilege of changing in
rooms that are far superior to the locker-room facilities assigned to the other athletes.) Each contestant,
upon entering and exiting the club's ivy-walled main
stadium—Centre Court—is asked to bow or curtsy
before the Royal Box, where the British monarchy
customarily sits.

*Ashe stretches for a backhand volley during an early-round match
at the 1975 All-England Championships at Wimbledon. Known
as an artful shotmaker and expert strategist, he reached the finals
in nearly one-third of all the open tournaments he entered.*

11

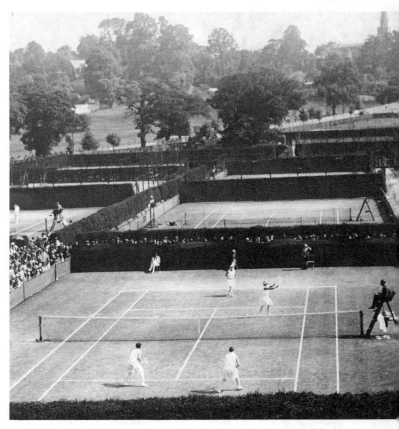

For nearly 100 years, the majority of the players who competed at Wimbledon were white and members of the upper class. Tennis, after all, had its roots as an exclusive, country club sport. Yet when Arthur Ashe walked onto Centre Court on the afternoon of July 5, 1975, to play in the tourney finals for the men's singles title, his main concerns were not Wimbledon's illustrious history, its myriad traditions, or even his desire to help break down racial barriers by becoming the first black to win the men's title. As he made his respectful bow to the Royal Box, Ashe was concentrating on how to beat his far younger and highly favored opponent, Jimmy Connors.

Ashe, who in 1968 had been ranked the number one player in the United States, was well known for

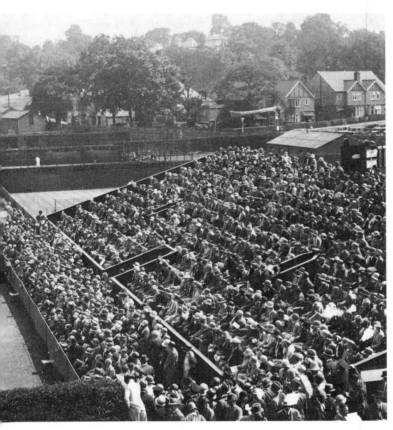

The All-England Lawn Tennis and Croquet Club, located in the London suburb of Wimbledon, has hosted the world's oldest tennis tournament, the All-England Championships, since 1877. Boasting such a long and extremely colorful history, Wimbledon is regarded as the event that most players desire to win above all others.

displaying an outwardly calm exterior while on the court, which gave some observers the impression that he did not care whether he won or lost his matches. Nevertheless, Ashe always possessed a burning desire to succeed, and as he warmed up for the start of the singles championship he remained in rapt concentration. He knew that beating Connors, the defending Wimbledon champion and a victor over Ashe in all three of their previous meetings, would demand his full attention.

The 22-year-old Connors, a self-taught southpaw from Belleville, Illinois, had burst onto the tennis scene only a couple of years earlier and was now taking the tennis world by storm. In fact, in 1975 he was coming off one of the best years any tennis player had ever experienced: 1974 had seen him win, in addition to Wimbledon, the U.S. Open, the Australian Open, and 12 other tournaments.

During the past two weeks at Wimbledon, Connors had certainly looked invincible. He had waltzed through each of his matches in the tournament without losing even one set. In his previous match, a semifinal showdown with Roscoe Tanner, Connors was particularly impressive, routing the hard-serving Tennessean 6–4, 6–1, 6–4.

Ashe, in contrast to the brash, mop-haired Connors, was pushing 32 and seemed past his prime. Although he still possessed a beautiful game to watch, smoothly blending a fearsome backhand and a deft touch with a knack for making spectacular shots, most observers thought he had played his best tennis years ago. And now that he was still recovering from a minor injury to his left heel, very few people gave him much of a chance to beat Connors.

To make matters even worse for Ashe, his seeding at Wimbledon had forced him to take a much tougher route to the finals than Jimmy Connors had followed. (In most tournaments, the top contestants are seeded, or placed in the draw, so that they will not meet each other in the early rounds.) Like Connors, Ashe had dispatched his first three opponents in the tournament with relative ease. But then he had hooked up against Sweden's Bjorn Borg in a grueling four-set match in the quarterfinals and had been stretched to five sets by Australian Tony Roche in the semifinals. By the time July 5 arrived, the London oddsmakers had installed Connors as an overwhelming 3-to-20 favorite to retain his Wimbledon title over the weary, injured Ashe.

Being the underdog was nothing new to Arthur Ashe. He was used to having the odds stacked against him. He had grown up in Richmond, Virginia, a southern city where racial segregation was enforced by local statutes known as Jim Crow laws. Barred from the city's better-equipped white facilities and institutions, blacks were kept "in their place" right from childhood, when they were denied access to Richmond's best schools and had the notion instilled in them that they could not hope to achieve the same things that whites could.

Ashe, however, chose to buck the odds, and he wound up doing so in a sport that had largely remained closed to blacks. Thanks to a massive parks program sponsored by the federal government, thousands of public courts were built across America in the 1930s. Nevertheless, the game did not catch on with the nation's black population. The United States Lawn Tennis Association (USLTA), the sport's governing body in America, remained reluctant to open up the sport to blacks and found ways to keep them from participating in USLTA events. Private tennis clubs, generally run by wealthy whites, refused to permit blacks to compete in major tournaments.

Even today, tennis is primarily a game for the privileged. The equipment is expensive, and court fees are often high. If Ashe had not grown up next to the tennis courts in Brook Field, a public recreation park in Richmond, it is very likely that he would never have learned to play the sport so well.

There was one other obstacle for Ashe to overcome during his youth: In spite of having free reign of the Brook Field courts, he often had trouble finding worthy competition. Almost all of the highly skilled players in the area were white, and they did not compete against blacks. As a result, Ashe made his way up the tennis ladder battling racism as skillfully as he played his opponents across the net.

By the time Ashe had made it to the top of the tennis world, racism was no longer a major problem faced by the sport's black players. Most whites had grown to respect black athletes. Ashe, for one, was often the crowd favorite.

Yet Ashe never forgot the lessons of his difficult youth, when he had to rely on his intelligence, self-discipline, and even temper to battle racial injustice. What was more, he drew frequently on these traits to help himself out of tough circumstances on the court. Such was the case when he prepared to play Connors at Wimbledon.

Ashe developed such a brilliant game plan that on the morning of the finals he told his good friend Dr. Doug Stein, "I have this funny feeling I can't lose." Ashe understood that he would probably lose if he let Connors dictate the tempo of the match. So, he decided to play away from Connors's greatest strength, counterpunching, even if that meant sacrificing some of his own strengths.

Normally a hard-hitting, fantastic shotmaker, Ashe chose to play very conservatively against Connors: He would concentrate on keeping the ball in play, even though that meant trying to hit fewer winners than usual. Ashe believed that Connors, who probably hit his forehand and backhand harder, more accurately, and with greater consistency than anyone in the sport, could not be outslugged. Instead, Ashe would have to outsavvy Connors and frustrate him into making errors.

On his serve, Ashe decided against hitting the ball hard and flat. He would twist the ball deep into the corner of the service court (the area into which the ball must be served), placing it at acute angles to pull Connors off the court. Ashe would then rush the net behind these sharply angled serves, more often than not putting himself in perfect position to volley Connors's return of serve into a wide-open court. (In tennis, a point may be won by either the server or the receiver, but among the top professionals the server has a tremendous advantage because he or she—initially, at least—controls the action. It is thus a significant feat to win an opponent's service game, an act known as *breaking service*.)

When Connors was serving, Ashe planned to draw him to the net with short chip shots and then lob the ball high over his head, forcing Connors to retreat. When not in a position to lob, Ashe would try to keep the ball low, so that Connors, who preferred to hit flat shots with very little spin, would have to swing up to get the ball over the net.

Another key tactic for Ashe was to contact the ball softly during a rally to force Connors to generate his own power. In doing so, Ashe also tried to avoid hitting the ball near the sidelines, both to increase his margin of error and to prevent Connors from hitting his customary, dangerously angled shots. Above all, Ashe wanted to control the rhythm of the game, keeping Connors off balance while forcing him to play in a style to which he was not accustomed.

Even though this defensive strategy marked a complete reversal from Ashe's usual game, which was to hit all out on almost every shot, he was convinced it would give him the greatest chance of pulling off an upset. But to accomplish this feat and play such a mannered style of tennis, Ashe would have to remain extremely disciplined and unemotional. This seemed a particularly difficult thing to do because in 1975 there was no love lost between Ashe and Connors.

Only days before the match, Connors had slapped Ashe with a $3 million lawsuit, charging him with libel. Connors had taken offense when Ashe had criticized him for taking part in high-paying "challenge matches"—which pit the game's best players against each other in one-day exhibitions—yet refusing to play on the U.S. Davis Cup team. Ashe had called Connors's refusal to join the squad "seemingly unpatriotic."

An intent Ashe on the morning of July 5, hours before the start of the 1975 men's singles championship at Wimbledon, prepares for his 2:00 P.M. showdown with Jimmy Connors. Ashe devised a game plan that called for an enormous amount of self-discipline because it required him to play defensive tennis rather than hit all out, as was his custom.

Jimmy Connors was the number one player in the world and the current titleholder at Wimbledon when he squared off against Ashe in the 1975 men's finals. "He'll make all the necessary sacrifices to win. He'll chase everything down," Ashe said of his hard-hitting opponent.

In Davis Cup competition, which features country against country, each participating nation seeks to field a squad of its very best players. Even though they are not paid for their services, most players regard it as a great honor to be asked to represent their country in Davis Cup competition. In 1975, Ashe was already a longtime veteran of Davis Cup play; he would later become captain of the U.S. squad. Connors, on the other hand, had decided that the Davis Cup was not for him and refused all invitations to join the U.S. team. Perhaps to needle him, Ashe had arived at Centre Court in his blue Davis Cup warm-up jacket, with the letters *USA* inscribed in red across the chest.

Also creating tension between Ashe and Connors was the latter's refusal to join the Association of Tennis Professionals (ATP). Ashe, the union's current president, had helped establish the organization several years earlier to protect the interests of tennis professionals around the world. Connors was one of the few top male players not to join the ATP.

"If we're not strong, the promoters will give us no choices," Ashe had once explained to Connors.

"I want to go my own way," Connors had responded. And so he did, filing 3 suits, totaling $20 million, against the ATP.

The media delighted in playing up the rivalry between Ashe, the underdog, and Connors, the defending champion, as the match drew near. Newspapers and magazines billed the 1975 Wimbledon finals as a battle between good and evil. Ashe, handsome and gentlemanly, with his famous studied cool, quickly became the crowd favorite; Connors was cast as the villain.

Ashe had long since earned the respect and admiration of most tennis fans by becoming the first black male to break the sport's racial barrier. Althea Gibson, winner of the 1957 and 1958 ladies' singles title at Wimbledon, had been the first black to cross the color line. But no great black male tennis players had followed her example and won a major tournament until Ashe came along.

Connors was a groundbreaker in an altogether different fashion. He was among the first of a generation of players to awe tennis fans with exceptional shotmaking while exhibiting abusive and sometimes childish behavior. At this early stage in his career, Connors was an ill-mannered bully who often screamed at linesmen and made obscene gestures at the spectators. A few years later, he cleaned up his act and became a crowd favorite in his own right. But at Wimbledon in 1975, the courtside fans were solidly behind Ashe when play began.

To win a game in tennis, a player must win four points—provided the margin of victory is two points or more. Tennis employs a unique scoring system: *Love* means that no points have been scored; *15* is used to indicate the first point won by each player; 30 denotes the second point scored; 40 means the third point. If the score is tied at 40–all, or *deuce*, the first player to capture the next point, called the *advantage*, as well as the point after that, wins the game; the score reverts to deuce if the player who holds the advantage fails to win the following point.

A player who wins six games (seven if the score is knotted at five–all) captures the *set*—provided the margin of victory is two games or more. In most tournaments since 1970, a tie-breaking system is invoked if the set reaches six games apiece. In such circumstances nowadays, the first player to score seven points in the *tie breaker* wins the set—provided the margin of victory is two points or more.

At Wimbledon (where a tie breaker is employed only in the fifth set), the first player to take three sets wins the match. So, when Ashe handily won the first 2 sets of the 1975 finals in a total of only 45 minutes, by a score of 6–1 in each set, he seemed to be coasting to an easy victory. His strategy was working to perfection: Connors, who had not lost a set all tournament long, was so off balance and confused that Ashe looked like he was playing against an amateur, not the world's top-ranked player. When a fan yelled out at one point, "Come on, Connors!" the reigning champion shot back, "I'm trying, for crissake!"

Still, Connors was a born fighter, and he was not going to let the match get away from him without putting up a terrific struggle. He clawed back and won the third set, 7–5. Then Connors broke Ashe's serve two games later and jumped out to a 3–0 lead in the fourth set. As the two players headed to the sidelines for a brief rest before a changeover (players switch sides of the court after every odd-numbered game in a set), the importance of the upcoming games was clear: If Connors were to hold onto his advantage and take the fourth set, he would even the match at

two sets apiece and carry tremendous momentum heading into the fifth and deciding set.

What happened during the next few moments proved to be the turning point of the match. Worried that his game plan was beginning to fail, Ashe felt tempted to abandon his carefully thought-out strategy and return to his normal style of play. "I had to decide whether or not to continue as is, or just blast back," he recalled in his autobiography *Off the Court*. "I decided to continue feeding him more junk, force him to the net and lob." Just when one of the most important matches of his life seemed to be slipping away, Ashe exercised an extraordinary amount of self-discipline, maintaining enough confidence to stick to his original strategy.

As Ashe rested in his chair, he looked calmly into his hands, just as he had done during each previous break in the action. This image, of the pensive Ashe staring transfixed at his hands, became one of the most memorable of the tournament. Many observers thought he was meditating. Actually, he was reading

Ashe lunges across the Centre Court grass to retrieve a sharply angled shot by Jimmy Connors during their 1975 title match at Wimbledon. According to Ashe, "If you're in a real tight match where the balance of power is almost even, winning shots may be a matter of inches and split seconds."

Ashe holds aloft his championship trophy moments after defeating Jimmy Connors in four sets, 6–1, 6–1, 5–7, 6–4, to capture the 1975 men's singles title at Wimbledon. Ashe remains the only black ever to play for and win the most prestigious event in men's tennis.

some notes he had made on small cards before the match; they were to remind him to follow through with his strategy.

The decision to continue feeding junk to Connors turned out to be the right one. Behind 3–0 in the fourth set, Ashe held his serve. He fought to deuce in the next game, then smashed an overhead for a chance to break Connors's serve; he raced across the court on the very next point and hit a forehand down the line for a winner to make the score 3–2. When Ashe won his service game, the set stood even at three games apiece.

In the next two games, each player held serve. Then Ashe broke Connors for a 5–4 lead and a chance to serve for the match. He won this game without losing a single point, concluding the match with a big serve that Connors could only lollipop over the net, setting up Ashe's final overhead smash.

Ashe has since been credited with playing one of the smartest tennis matches in Wimbledon history. His strategy has been likened to boxing champion Muhammad Ali's tactics for beating George Foreman for the heavyweight title in Zaire the previous year. In that fight, Ali had assumed a defensive posture, covering his face with his hands, and had let Foreman punch away until he became frustrated and tired. In much the same way, Ashe had refused to give Connors shots with any pace on them. He had played brilliant defensive tennis.

It was not until many years later that the full impact of Ashe's stunning victory could be fairly measured. Heading into the 1975 finals, Connors had been picking up steam on his way to becoming the world's most dominant player. If he had beaten Ashe at Wimbledon, there is no telling how far he would have gone. But Ashe, with his victory, showed Connors's subsequent opponents a good way to play him and in doing so helped shape the course of professional tennis for the next decade. Connors was forced to share the tennis spotlight in the late 1970s and early 1980s with other great players, such as Bjorn Borg, John McEnroe, Ivan Lendl, and, for a few more years, Ashe himself.

For Ashe, the victory over Connors was easily among the most satisfying of his career. When he slammed the final ball away to win the prestigious tournament, he gave way to the emotion of the moment. In an uncharacteristic public display of feeling, Ashe turned to the box where his friends and advisers sat, raised his fist in victory, and relished his great win. "When I took the match point," he explained later, "all the years, all the effort, all the support I had received over the years came together. It's a long way from Brook Field to Wimbledon."

2

"THE LITTLE BOY WHO COULD PLAY TENNIS"

ARTHUR ROBERT ASHE, Jr., was born on July 10, 1943, at St. Phillips, a hospital for blacks in Richmond, Virginia. He lived with his parents at an uncle's house until he was four years old. Then came one of the most important changes in his life.

In 1947, the city of Richmond hired his father, Arthur, Sr., as a special police officer in charge of its biggest playground, the 18-acre Brook Field. (The elder Ashe had previously been a jack-of-all-trades, working as a chauffeur, gardener, and carpenter. Because he usually held two or three of these jobs at the same time, the Ashes always managed to live comfortably.) With this new post came a five-room frame house at 1610 Sledd Street, in the middle of the blacks-only playground. A five-minute walk separated the family from their nearest neighbors.

Arthur, Jr., for one, did not complain about the move. Brook Field contained four hard-surface tennis courts and a backboard to hit balls against as well as an Olympic-size swimming pool, basketball courts, and baseball diamonds. It was a sports-lover's paradise.

The budding tennis star at age 12, outside his Brook Field home in Richmond, Virginia. A public recreation park, Brook Field was, he said, "my whole universe" throughout much of his childhood.

Arthur first picked up a tennis racket when he was about six years old. "My arms and legs were thin as soda straws," he wrote in his autobiography *Advantage Ashe*. "But I soon began to be good at the game, maybe because I was born with extra-quick reflexes." Before long, he became known around the courts, he said, "as 'the little boy who could play tennis.' "

Tennis was not Arthur's only love, however. His mother, Mattie—or Baby, as she was known to her family—coddled her first son (her second child, John, was born in 1948) and taught him to read even before he entered the Baker Street elementary school. "Many days as a kid I'd turn on soft music and read all day," Ashe recalled. An excellent student, he invariably got straight A's and was elected president of his class when he was in the sixth grade.

When Arthur was not reading—*National Geographic* was always a great favorite—or playing sports in his spare time, he was usually kept busy by his father. A kindhearted man but also a strict disciplinarian, the senior Ashe demanded a great deal of his sons. The Ashe boys were not allowed to hang around after school with their friends; they had to be home 10 minutes after the final bell rang to pitch in with the chores, which usually included chopping wood and helping take care of Brook Field and its facilities. Arthur, Jr., and John eventually learned as much about running the park as their father could teach them.

Whatever Daddy Ashe said, went—no questions asked. There was to be no talking back or showing any disrespect to adults; the Ashe boys were taught to be extremely polite. Arthur, Sr., exacted harsh punishment when his children did not listen to him. His eldest son still remembers the long, thick belt with which his father administered whippings.

An even more powerful memory surrounds a Saturday morning in March 1950. Mattie Ashe was having trouble with her third pregnancy and was scheduled to check into St. Phillips Hospital. (Her eldest son still retains a vivid image of her wearing a blue corduroy bathrobe while standing in the doorway of their house that morning, about to go off to the hospital.) She was supposed to have minor surgery, but complications developed after the operation and she suffered a fatal case of toxemia, a condition in which the blood pressure increases abnormally. Daddy Ashe immediately broke down and cried when he returned from the hospital on the morning of her death. "This is all I got left," he kept repeating as he clutched his two sons.

Arthur, Jr., feeling his world turned inside out, chose not to attend his mother's funeral. After giving her one last kiss as she lay in her coffin in the middle of his family's living room, he went to a neighbor's yard and watched from a distance as the mourners made their way to the Westwood Baptist Church.

Shortly after Mattie Ashe's death, Arthur's father hired Mrs. Otis Berry, a patient, loving, elderly widow, to help raise the two boys. It took Arthur a long time to accept Mrs. Berry as a substitute mother, but he eventually came to realize that she was trying her hardest to take care of the family.

Arthur gained a second substitute mother in March 1955, when his father married Lorene Kimbrough. She and her two children, Robert and Loretta, moved into the house on Sledd Street, prompting Mrs. Berry to share a room with Arthur and John. Ordinarily, this arrangement would have made things a bit awkward, but by then the adolescent Ashe had begun to spend long periods away from home, playing tennis.

Arthur did not possess the build one would expect of a future world-class athlete. He had experienced a disease-ridden childhood, contracting the measles, mumps, whooping cough, chicken pox, and diphtheria. These and many other illnesses had left him

Arthur Ashe, Sr., worked hard to instill in his eldest son the self-reliance and self-discipline that would serve him well both on and off the court. "The inequities imposed by racism were frustrating," Arthur, Jr., said of his boyhood years, "but I was fortunate to be surrounded by a devoted father and other black people determined to push me along, broaden my horizons, and help me develop a sense of myself that ignored the limits white Richmond wanted to impose at the time."

slight and not particularly strong. Accordingly, he was too small while he was growing up to excel in any sports but baseball—his greatest love at the time—and tennis. "Sometimes, from a distance, I'd watch white kids playing on the 16 courts of Byrd Park, where it was illegal for me to set foot," he remembered in *Advantage Ashe*. "I learned from watching, and got to like the game more and more."

Despite his growing interest in the sport, Arthur might never have taken up tennis seriously were it not for Ronald Charity, a student at nearby Virginia Union University and one of the top black tennis players in the nation. Charity, who had taught himself the game with the help of several how-to books and a borrowed racket, spent his summers polishing his strokes at Brook Field, where he had a part-time job as a tennis instructor.

Arthur used to watch Charity practice his graceful swing from a distance, until one day the collegian introduced himself to the seven year old and offered to teach him the game. Thereafter, Charity spent many hours working with his young student, first showing him the proper grip to be used by a beginning player and then tirelessly throwing balls to Arthur's forehand and backhand and correcting his strokes. When Charity was not around, Arthur spent countless hours by himself hitting a ball against a backboard to perfect his swing.

Charity saw that Arthur had talent from the start. Even though he was playing with a cheap racket that was far too big and heavy for him, the young Ashe learned the game quickly and easily. When he was eight years old, he entered a tournament held on the Brook Field courts and lost to a boy who was three years older. The loss did not deter him, however. "I liked the taste of competition," Ashe remembered. "I entered tournaments at other Negro parks in Richmond, and began winning."

One of Arthur's most important lessons took place when he played against a youth his own age. "He kept looking around after he hit good shots, to see who might have been watching," Charity said of Ashe. "I bawled him out for it. I told him if he continued to do anything like that I wasn't going to be bothered with him anymore." Ashe immediately stopped gloating.

Arthur had developed into a very solid player by the time he was almost 10 years old. Still small and thin, he shocked a number of stronger and older youths when he won Brook Field's local tournament. But the victory came as no surprise to Ashe. Under Charity's watchful eye, he had been improving his game by playing against grown-ups at the Richmond Racquet Club.

By 1953, Charity decided that if Arthur's talent was to be properly nurtured, the youngster required a much more experienced coach. And Charity had just the person in mind: Dr. Robert Walter Johnson, who in addition to being a successful medical doctor was an avid tennis fan, an excellent player, and an accomplished teacher. Johnson had not discovered the game of tennis until he was in his mid-thirties, but he quickly became obsessed with it and built a court at his Lynchburg, Virginia, home. He soon became a good enough player to win seven mixed-doubles titles with his protégée Althea Gibson at the national championships of the American Tennis Association (ATA), the black counterpart of the USLTA.

When Johnson retired from competition, he made it his mission to promote the game among young blacks by taking promising players into his home during the summer and coaching them. Along with instructing these youngsters for a couple of weeks at a time, he took them on the road to play in tournaments. Most of these students, whom he called his

Junior Development Team, could not afford to pay their way, so Johnson took care of all their expenses.

In the spring of 1953, the Central Intercollegiate Athletic Association (CIAA), an organization of black colleges, held a tennis tournament at Virginia Union University. It was there that Charity introduced Arthur to Johnson, who watched the soon-to-be 10 year old hit some balls during a break between matches. "All right, Ronald," Johnson said to Ashe's mentor. "I'll take him for a while, if you want to carry him up [to Lynchburg]." When the idea was presented to Daddy Ashe, he agreed to let his son go to Johnson's house for two weeks that summer. "Without any of us knowing it at the time," Ashe said later, "Daddy and Ronald and Johnson set my feet on the long trail that led out of Richmond to the white tournament circuit."

For the rest of the spring, Arthur looked forward to his summer visit. The opportunity to play tennis all day long and perhaps travel to a few tournaments excited him. But staying at Johnson's large three-story house was not at all like going to a tennis camp. Ashe, along with three other boys and two girls who were there, had to work for their keep, tending to Johnson's spacious grounds, taking care of his hunting dogs, and maintaining the tennis court.

The labor posed no problem for Arthur, the youngest member of the Junior Development Team; thanks to his father's demands, he was used to hard work. But he did encounter other troubles. Johnson's ideas about how the game should be played were different from Charity's, and the 10 year old was reluctant to change his habits. When Johnson's son, Bobby, told Arthur to change his grip on his backhand and to shorten his stroke, he refused to listen to his new teacher. "Mr. Charity showed me the other way," Arthur said stubbornly.

Johnson promptly phoned the senior Ashe in Richmond, who hopped in his Ford and made the

three-hour trip to Lynchburg. "Dr. Johnson is teaching you now, Arthur Junior," Daddy Ashe told his son. "You do everything he says, no matter what he tells you." After that brief talk, there were never again any problems between the young Ashe and Johnson.

Arthur made use of several devices to sharpen his fundamentals during his stay in Lynchburg. In Johnson's garage, there was a tennis ball suspended by a vertical cord, enabling a budding player to get a better feel for his strokes by hitting the ball with a racket-length broom handle. There was also a service stand for holding a ball in place while practicing serves; a ball-spewing Ball-Boy machine; a rebounding net; and a backboard. Arthur took his turn on all of these pieces of equipment—and then some. "Sometimes the neighbors would complain about my pounding

Dr. Robert Walter Johnson (right) and his son, Bobby (left), worked with Ashe every summer from 1953 to 1960 to improve his tennis game. In addition to learning the finer points of the sport at the Johnsons' home, Ashe said that he was "schooled in the strictest manners and taught an unshakable oriental calm."

the backboard at 7 A.M.," he said in *Off the Court*. "But by the time breakfast came around, I had put in a good forty-five minutes."

Drills were also a big part of Arthur's day in Lynchburg. "We had to hit so many down the line," he recalled, "so many cross-court, maybe a cross-court then a down-the-line, come to the net and put away the volley. We had daily contests: who could hit the most forehands without an error, the most forehand returns of serve, deep forehand shots, forehand approach shots, forehand passing shots. Then we ran through the whole series for the backhand." When Johnson's youngsters went up against the Ball-Boy machine, he made them hit the same stroke 100 times. "I believe in practice," he told them.

On top of all that physical effort, Arthur read every book on tennis strategy in Johnson's library. He learned to aim down the line on approach shots and when to attempt other kinds of shots. Not as strong as the other boys, he also discovered the importance of being a hard-nosed, consistent player. Because he did not hit his serve and ground strokes as sharply as his opponents did, he concentrated on keeping the ball in play until they made a mistake.

Another type of lesson offered by Johnson focused on court etiquette. Anxious to have his players make inroads in the white tennis world, Johnson wanted them to avoid racial confrontations of any kind. As a result, he taught the Junior Development Team members to keep their composure when they got angry, to call their opponent's shots "in" when there was any doubt about them being out-of-bounds, and to pick up all the balls on their side of the court before changing sides so they could hand the balls to their opponent. "There will *be* some cheating," Johnson used to say. "But we aren't going to do it."

These lessons on good manners extended to the world beyond the court. When Johnson and his players traveled to distant tournaments, in places such as Baltimore, Maryland, and Washington, D.C., they often wound up staying as guests in someone's home. On these occasions, Johnson expected his protégés to be perfectly behaved ladies and gentlemen. "I want you to be accepted without being a center of attraction," he told them.

Arthur learned these lessons extremely well. Indeed, the self-discipline that Johnson demanded of Arthur stayed with him for the remainder of his career. On the court, he was always cool, composed, and completely in control of himself.

One day, when Arthur was playing in a tournament in Norfolk, Virginia, he took these lessons to an extreme. Comfortably ahead in the second set after having won the first, he decided to be a good sport and take it easy against his young, clearly overmatched opponent. Arthur wound up losing the second set as well as the third, which gave the match to the other youngster. From that moment on, Arthur resolved to always give his best effort and to never let his emotions affect his play.

The next summer, Arthur returned to Johnson's home—he would head there every summer until he was 18—and the dividends of his hard work soon began to pay off: He triumphed in the 12-and-under division of every tournament in which Johnson entered him. The following year, 1955, Arthur took his climb to the top of boys' tennis one step further: He traveled to Durham, North Carolina, and won the ATA National Championship for boys 12 years and under. He went on to win the ATA's 15-and-under title in 1957, when he was 14, and he captured the title again the following year.

Johnson entered Arthur in several predominantly white tournaments during the summer of 1958. The 15 year old reached the semifinals of the New Jersey Boys' Tournament, topped a field of 150 players to win the Maryland Junior Tournament, and put up a good showing at the National Boys' Championships in Kalamazoo, Michigan. But when Johnson attempted to enter Arthur in a junior tournament in his hometown of Richmond, the Middle Atlantic chapter of the USLTA refused to accept the black teenager's application. Still, he could take some comfort in that the USLTA now ranked him fifth among all boys in the nation. Just as satisfying, he had recently beaten Ronald Charity in an ATA tournament.

Arthur's athletic talent did not go unnoticed at Maggie Walker High School, where he made the varsity baseball team in his sophomore year and was named the tennis team's number one player. Immediately after Arthur pitched in his first ball game, however, the school's principal, J. Harry Williams, advised him to give up playing baseball, saying that Arthur's future as a tennis player was too promising for him to focus half his attention on another sport. Rather reluctantly, the high school sophomore agreed to end his baseball career.

It was a wise decision. Arthur earned a national ranking of 44th among juniors in 1959, and the following year he won both the ATA's junior and men's singles titles, becoming the latter tournament's youngest champion ever. In 1960, he also teamed up in the ATA's junior doubles with his 12-year-old brother, John, but failed to come away with the trophy. (John nevertheless won the doubles title two years later.)

By the time Arthur was getting ready to begin his senior year in school, it was apparent that he was the best young black player since Althea Gibson. But because of his tremendous progress, another decision awaited the 17-year-old Ashe. If he wanted to continue improving, he would have to be able to play tennis year-round.

Both Daddy Ashe and Johnson realized that Arthur had outgrown Richmond. "Anybody, white or Negro, who had a strong tennis game had to get out of Virginia if he wanted to keep climbing," the tennis star said later. Arthur could not play winter tennis there; no indoor courts were available to blacks. What was more, he had no one to compete against. He was head and shoulders above every other player in the area. The best local white player in his age group was O. H. Parrish, but because Richmond was a racially segregated city, the two never squared off against each another until 1961, when Arthur beat him in Wheeling, West Virginia, to take the Middle Atlantic Juniors Championship.

Accordingly, Arthur was sent out of the South, to Sumner High School in St. Louis, Missouri. There he played tennis indoors during the winter and com-

Ashe (second from left) poses with a group of Dr. Johnson's protégés. Johnson referred to these youngsters, whom he trained and entered in regional tournaments, as his Junior Development Team.

peted against such top players as Cliff and Butch Buchholz and Chuck McKinley. He lived in St. Louis with one of Johnson's good friends, Richard Hudlin, a tennis lover and former captain of the University of Chicago tennis team.

Spending a year away from Virginia proved to be a tonic for Arthur's game. When the weather was warm, he practiced on the outdoor courts at nearby Washington University. At other times, he played indoors, at the 138th Infantry Armory. The Armory's slick, fast wood floors encouraged Arthur, whose game had been fashioned around steady ground strokes, to develop a more aggressive, powerful style. With the help of Larry Miller, the Armory pro, he shortened his backswing, learned to take the ball on the rise, added some wallop to his serve, and began to rush the net more often. The small, skinny kid who used to try to outlast his competitors from the baseline was on the verge of becoming one of the pioneers of serve-and-volley tennis.

Arthur's other pursuits in St. Louis were just as rewarding. He was admittedly shy while growing up in Richmond; between reading, studying, doing chores, and practicing tennis, he never had as much of a chance to socialize as he would have liked. But at Sumner High, the studious Ashe found it easier to be more outgoing when he went out on dates; because he had been brought to the city to play sports, his peers had imbued him with a kind of star status. All the while, he continued to excel in the classroom and graduated with the highest grade point average in the school.

Nevertheless, Arthur's most satisfying moment during the school year occurred, predictably enough, on the tennis court. On his way to the National Juniors Indoor tourney in November 1960, he thought about Johnson's long-standing goal: to see a black schoolboy compete successfully with whites and win a major USLTA event. Johnson had been sending members of his Junior Development Team to tournaments for years, but none had ever come out on top. The 17-year-old Ashe changed all that by upsetting the top seed, 19-year-old Frank Froehling, in a 4¼-hour marathon in the finals, 6–1, 16–14, 9–11, 3–6, 6–1. At that point, he said later, "It was the biggest thrill in my life."

The following month, Arthur traveled to Miami Beach, Florida, to compete in the Orange Bowl Juniors, then headed north to Richmond to spend the Christmas holidays with his family. On the very day he arrived at home, he received a phone call from J. D. Morgan, coach of the men's tennis team at the University of California, Los Angeles (UCLA). What Morgan wanted to tell Arthur Ashe would lift the teenager's spirits even higher.

3

A RISING STAR

Ashe practices his forehand volley at the University of California, Los Angeles (UCLA), where he enrolled in the fall of 1961. "Of course, there was a great deal of fuss about being the 'first black' Junior Davis Cup player, the 'first black' to get a tennis scholarship to UCLA," he said. "The fact that this kind of accomplishment by a black player got so much attention was an indication that we still had so far to go."

J. D. MORGAN first saw Arthur Ashe play tennis in 1958, at the National Boys' Championships in Kalamazoo. After watching the teenager's progress over the next two years, the UCLA coach decided by the end of 1960 to offer him an athletic scholarship—the first one ever extended by the school to a black tennis player. The high school senior would eventually receive offers from the Hampton Institute, the University of Arizona, the University of Michigan, and Michigan State. But he had little trouble settling on UCLA, which possessed one of the top tennis programs in the nation. About his initial phone call from Morgan, he recalled in *Advantage Ashe*, "It was a short conversation. I just said, 'Don't worry, I'll be there.' "

At the time of the phone call, classes for incoming freshmen at UCLA were still nine months away. Ashe concentrated in the interim on finishing high school and improving his tennis game. He won his second major title, the National Interscholastics, in May 1961 and reached the semifinals of the National Jaycees and National Juniors tournaments. He became the fifth-ranked junior in America and was a member of the U.S. Junior Davis Cup team by the time he graduated from high school. (Mainly an honorary group, the Junior Davis Cup squad competes informally against teams from other countries.) He also won both the ATA men's singles and doubles (with Ronald Charity) titles. In an era in which teenagers did not dominate the tennis scene as many of them do today, Ashe also established himself as the 28th-ranked amateur in the nation.

By the end of the summer, Ashe was eager to begin a new chapter in his life. "When I decided to leave Richmond," he wrote in *Off the Court,* "I left all that Richmond stood for at the time—its segregation, its conservatism, its parochial thinking, its slow progress toward equality, its lack of opportunity for talented black people. I had no intention then of coming back." Although he retains fond memories of his childhood home and the loving relatives and friends who helped prepare him for his adult life, he has since returned to Richmond only for family visits and to play in local tournaments.

Ashe entered UCLA with the desire to get as much out of school academically and socially as he could. (He was engaged for a brief time in his senior year but did not go through with the marriage.) He intended to study either architecture or engineering, both very tough disciplines. Coach Morgan convinced him, however, to switch to a less demanding major, business administration, to accommodate his busy schedule, which included not only tennis but Reserve Officers' Training Corps (ROTC). Every freshman and sophomore male at UCLA was required to take ROTC. After that, he could either drop out of the program or take two more years of ROTC and serve in the military after college.

Ashe harbored no great ambitions to make a career for himself in the army. Still, he believed it was in his best interest to complete the program because he would most likely be drafted by the army after

UCLA tennis coach J. D. Morgan (left) offers a few words of instruction to Ashe. "Tennis is a difficult game to learn," Ashe observed. "You have to become adept in about four or five different sets of exercises, none of which are the same. Physiologically, serving a tennis ball is nothing like hitting a forehand; they're two completely different actions. Hitting a volley is not like hitting an overhead; they too are two completely different functions. You must learn how to do them all."

graduation. By remaining in ROTC, he would assure himself of becoming an officer rather than an ordinary soldier.

With so many activities to pursue, there never seemed to be enough time for Ashe to do everything he wanted to. No matter whether he was trying to polish his strokes or was hooked up in, as he put it, "another of the thousands of matches I've played," he would find his attention drifting to other subjects. His trouble with focusing on his game left some observers with the impression that he was not competitive enough to be a champion, that he was not a fighter. But Ashe's critics would soon find out that he could grit out tough victories as well as anyone.

The scholarship that UCLA awarded Ashe required him to put in 250 hours of work each year around the campus. That meant taking care of the tennis courts, a small price to pay for the opportunity to receive a first-rate education while training with

Charlie Pasarell, whom Ashe called his "closest buddy" on the juniors circuit and the U.S. Junior Davis Cup team, enrolled at UCLA in 1961, the same year that Ashe did, and subsequently became his roommate. "He and I were about even in tennis while we were at UCLA," Ashe said of Pasarell, "and sometimes he beat me out for the number one slot on the team."

one of the nation's top coaches. Besides, having to work for his keep was nothing new to Ashe.

Playing tennis on a top university team proved to be a much greater challenge, for Ashe was accustomed to being the best player wherever he was stationed. In high school and at Dr. Johnson's, he was clearly without peer. But at UCLA, he started out as the school's number three player, behind Charlie Pasarell, the National Juniors champion, and Dave Reed, who held the Southern California juniors title. Ashe managed to reap huge benefits from this situation, however. Because the top college programs recruited the best juniors from around the world, playing tennis for the UCLA Bruins gave him the opportunity to practice against high-level competition on a regular basis for the first time in his life.

Ashe had befriended the Puerto Rican–born Pasarell on the juniors tour, and they grew even closer during their university days. Coach Morgan also proved to be someone the 18-year-old Ashe could rely on. A few weeks after the school year began, the Balboa Bay Club in Orange County hosted a tournament of college teams that included UCLA. The club failed to invite Ashe, however, because it did not admit blacks.

California, Ashe realized, was not the paradise of equal opportunity he had imagined it to be. Pasarell softened the blow somewhat by staying out of the tournament in a show of support for his friend. Morgan, in fact, offered to hold the entire team out of the tournament as an act of protest, but Ashe decided not to make waves. After conferring with his coach, he felt it would be better to wait and make an issue of things when he was better established and his name carried more weight. Ashe followed through on his promise a few years later, when the Balboa Bay Club, he said, "decided I was good enough to be accepted." He adamantly refused all their invitations.

During his initial year at UCLA, Ashe often relied on his superior athletic talent to cover up for any lack of concentration and managed to post an undefeated season as a freshman. Morgan was a great motivator and helped the budding tennis star get the best out of his ability. But Morgan was not the only person who helped Ashe improve his game. Richard ("Pancho") Gonzales, one of the top players during the 1950s and 1960s, became another of his mentors.

The dark-skinned Gonzales, the reigning pro at the nearby Beverly Hills Tennis Club, had been one of Ashe's early idols. The Los Angeles native had played at a Richmond tournament years earlier, and his powerful game had impressed the young Ashe, who identified with Gonzales, partly because his dark skin made him look as though he were black. (He was actually of Mexican descent.) When Ashe was at UCLA, he often went to the Beverly Hills Tennis Club to watch Gonzales play. Eventually, he wound up as one of his boyhood hero's practice partners and received valuable pointers from the old master along the way.

Ashe, however, was quickly becoming a star in his own right. During his sophomore year, he won the Southern California sectional title and with it an automatic entry into the singles draw of the 1963 All-England Championships at Wimbledon. But being 1 of only 128 men to qualify for the world's most prestigious tournament was only half the battle as far as Ashe was concerned. He also had to find a way to scrape enough money together to cover the cost of the trip overseas.

That April, Ashe and Pasarell played an exhibition match at the California Club in West Los Angeles. Afterward, one of the club members, a woman named Julianna Ogner, stopped by and asked Ashe what his tennis plans were for the summer. He told her that he would be competing at Wimbledon if he could come up with the money to cover his plane fare and other expenses. Five minutes later, Ogner returned with the $800 Ashe needed to finance his trip. "I was so stunned I could barely stammer my thanks," he recalled in *Off the Court*. This unexpected act of generosity, by a white woman he barely knew, helped blot out the ugly memory of his being snubbed by the Balboa Bay Club.

Shortly before Ashe headed to Wimbledon in late June, he accompanied the UCLA team to Princeton, New Jersey, for the National Collegiate Athletic As-

"There's something electric about him," Ashe said of Richard *("Pancho")* Gonzalez, the top professional player from 1953 to 1961. *"He's always been my idol and, after a fashion, always will be."* Gonzalez, who used his combination of speed, coordination, and skill to make the game of tennis look effortless, joined the ranks of Ashe's courtside mentors in the early 1960s.

sociation (NCAA) championships. The tournament finale turned into a repeat of the Bruins' match earlier that spring against their crosstown rivals, the University of Southern California (USC) Trojans. But when USC came out on top this time, it was to claim the national championship. Ashe made it as far as the semifinals in the NCAA men's singles before he bowed in five sets to the powerful serve-and-volley game of the Trojans' Dennis Ralston, the eventual champ.

Ashe did not remain disappointed by his defeat for long; the following day, he boarded a plane bound for England—his first trip abroad. All told, his experiences overseas played out like a fantasy. As was the custom of the day at Wimbledon, a luxurious Bentley picked him up at his London hotel and drove him to the All-England Lawn Tennis and Croquet Club for each match. "The umpires wore hard straw hats and carnations just as they did in 1880," Ashe recalled. "There was green everywhere—green ivy, green canopies, green doors and balconies and chairs. . . . All the magnificence and efficiency dazed me a little."

But not too much. Ashe disposed of his first opponent, a Brazilian named Carlos Fernandes, in straight sets; the American's serve-and-volley skills clearly left Fernandes overmatched. Ashe's next adversary, the Australian John Hillebrand, put up a much tougher struggle; it took Ashe five sets to defeat him. The third round pitted Ashe against one of his rivals on the juniors circuit: Chuck McKinley, now a student at Trinity University in Texas and America's top player. Ashe lost in straight sets to McKinley, who wound up winning the tournament without losing a set.

Ashe followed his strong showing at Wimbledon with another series of impressive performances in a tournament in Budapest, Hungary. There he reached the semifinals before losing in five sets to Denmark's Torben Ulrich.

Ashe's overall efforts in Europe did a great deal to improve his standing in the tennis world. He had entered UCLA as the 28th-ranked amateur player in the United States. Now, after his first two years of college, he had advanced to number six.

Among Ashe's first stops after returning from Europe was the U.S. Hardcourt Championships in Chicago, Illinois. His game had come a long way since his days at Dr. Johnson's, when he usually tried to outlast his opponent on each point. He now possessed a bullet-fast serve and an incredibly hard backhand to accompany his very aggressive style.

Because of his dependence on power, Ashe had become a more effective player on faster surfaces, such as grass and cement, than on clay. Players who hit the ball hard excel on fast surfaces because their shots bounce off the court with a lot of pace and give their opponents little chance to stroke the ball properly. On clay, a deliberate, steady game is more effective than one built around power; when a hard-hit ball strikes the clay, the receiver has much more time to prepare for the shot than he or she does on a fast surface. Ashe showed that his game was ideally suited to fast surfaces by posting a convincing victory over Chris Crawford in the finals of the U.S. Hardcourts.

The UCLA sophomore's strong play in Chicago helped him land a place on the U.S. Davis Cup squad on August 1, along with Ralston, McKinley, and Marty Riessen. The invitation left Ashe exhilarated. "I had been a Davis Cup fan all my life," he said. He made his first Davis Cup appearance a successful one by defeating Orlando Bracamonte of Venezuela in straight sets in Denver, Colorado. Ashe was unable to remain on the squad and play in the United States's subsequent matches, however, because he had to return to Los Angeles for his junior year.

While Ashe was in the process of becoming a public figure, he was asked every so often by other black students at UCLA and members of the black media what he was doing to help the black community. "You can do clinics—and I've done my share—but you can never do enough," he said later. "They want you to be great as well as spend your free

time in the black community, and you can't do both. You can't be No. 1 on a tennis court and spend all your time in the black community." He would devote himself more fully to the plight of blacks later in his career.

In the meantime, Ashe's next two semesters at UCLA went by without a hitch. "As one of the ten top-ranking players in the country," he wrote in *Advantage Ashe*, "I got more and more invitations to travel here and there for exhibitions, with all expenses paid. J. D. [Morgan] encouraged me to accept some of these for the sake of getting more experience against the very best players."

By the time the 1964 season began, Ashe had become the top player at UCLA and the sixth-ranked

Coach J. D. Morgan (center) holds the team trophy awarded to the 1965 national collegiate champions, a UCLA squad that featured (from left to right) Ian Crookenden, Dave Sanderlin, Dave Reed, and Ashe. The plaques displayed by Ashe are for his capturing the men's singles and doubles titles.

amateur in the nation. USC's Dennis Ralston was the only higher-ranking Californian, and like their two schools, Ashe and Ralston developed quite a rivalry. Ashe edged out Ralston in the Southern California Intercollegiate Tournament, 4–6, 6–4, 8–6. Ralston took his revenge in the Southern California Sectional Championship and the Big Six Intercollegiate Tournament.

Ashe returned to the grass circuit as soon as the school year ended. He went to Wimbledon in June and made it to the fourth round before losing in straight sets to the eventual champion, Roy Emerson. Back in the States, Ashe entered the Eastern Grass Court Championships, in South Orange, New Jersey, whose field included 6 of the top 10 American players.

He breezed through the early rounds, then found himself in a tough match against a familiar foe, Dennis Ralston, in the quarterfinals.

Ralston outlasted Ashe in the first set, 15–13, but the UCLA star came back strong to capture the following two sets and the match. Up next was a meeting with the tournament's defending champion, Gene Scott, who had knocked Ashe out of the tourney the previous year. This time around, Ashe won in straight sets to reach the finals, where the hard-hitting Clark Graebner awaited him. Ashe had his serve broken in the first set, but he did not lose another service game all day. His subsequent 4–6, 6–4, 6–4, 6–3 victory gave him the first major grass-court title of his career.

Next on Ashe's summer schedule was America's most prestigious tournament, the U.S. National Championships, at the West Side Tennis Club in Forest Hills, New York. He had made his first appearance on the Forest Hills grass courts in 1959, losing in the first round to one of the sport's all-time greats, Rod Laver. Ashe had played there every year since then, and in 1964 he made his best showing ever, battling his way to the fourth round before losing to Tony Roche.

"It is not the speed of grass that does a guy in, but the unpredictability," Ashe observed in his book *Arthur Ashe: Portrait in Motion.* "A couple of guys can hit for four hours on clay, but you will come off a two-hour grass match more fatigued because you are so much more mentally spent. This is especially true at Forest Hills where the courts are significantly more uneven than at Wimbledon. You can never stop concentrating at Forest Hills, or you're dead."

Ashe's crowning achievement in 1964 took place off the court, when he was named the winner of the Johnston Award, given each year to the American tennis player who contributes the most to the growth of the sport while exhibiting good sportsmanship and character. This honor not only attested to Ashe's many positive qualities but revealed that the tennis establishment, which for years had been ruled by the wealthy, white country club set, had at last accepted blacks.

Ashe, who ended 1964 with an amateur ranking of number three in the United States, joked upon accepting the award, "I hope I can prove to be the exception to the rule that good guys always finish last." As it turned out, he would not have to wait all that long for his chance. ❦

4

"I MIGHT LICK ANYBODY"

AS I STARTED into 1965," Athur Ashe wrote in *Advantage Ashe*, "I knew it was a make-or-break year for me." It proved to be his best year yet.

Ashe's good fortune began with his being asked by the new U.S. Davis Cup captain, George McCall, to compete against Canada in the American zone's semifinal round in Bakersfield, California. (The countries that take part in this international team event are placed into specific zones, with the winner of each zone advancing into the next round. To triumph in each round, or *tie*, of Davis Cup competition, a nation must win at least three matches. A tie consists of four singles and one doubles contest.) Ashe took the court in two of the matches and beat both Keith Carpenter and Harry Fauquier in straight sets to help the United States advance into the zone's final round, to be held later that summer against Mexico.

Ashe finished out the school year in the meantime, and he did it in grand style. In June, he won the NCAA singles titles and captured the doubles titles with Ian Crookenden. At the age of 21, Ashe was able to lay claim to being the top collegiate player in the nation.

Ashe launches his 6-foot 1-inch, 155-pound body into his serve during the 1965 U.S. Nationals at the West Side Tennis Club in Forest Hills, New York. "To reach the top rank in the world," he said, "you cannot just be very good and very consistent. You must have at least one outstanding stroke. I have two very reliable shots—my serve and my backhand."

Ashe looked to continue his hot streak at Wimbledon, where he won his first three matches before falling to Rafael Osuna of Mexico, 8–6, 6–4, 6–4, on June 26. Ashe soon got a chance to avenge the loss. Despite some ragged play after Wimbledon, he was again asked to play on the U.S. Davis Cup team, in its showdown against Mexico in Dallas, Texas. As the pairings would have it, the first match of the competition pitted Ashe against Osuna.

Unlike at Wimbledon, Ashe was at the top of his game in Dallas. His booming serve was too powerful for the versatile Mexican—Ashe served 15 aces (serves that one's opponent fails to touch) during the match—and his ground strokes were crisp and effective. He blanketed Osuna 6–2, 6–3, 9–7. Then he beat Antonio Palafox convincingly two days later— Ashe served four straight aces in one game—to help the United States advance to the interzone finals against Spain. This tie was to be held in Barcelona on slow clay courts, hardly Ashe's favorite surface, so he was not asked to represent his country in spite of having posted a 5–0 record so far in Davis Cup competition.

Characteristically, Ashe took the slight in stride and quickly turned his attention to tennis's next major event: the U.S. Nationals. He entered Forest Hills as the fifth seed and made it all the way to the quarterfinal round on September 10, only to face the number one seed and the top-ranked amateur player in the world since 1962, Roy Emerson, on the Marquee Court. Ashe, who was not expected to do much more than put up a good fight, decided to gamble in his approach to the match. He would not just return the Australian's serve but would attack it, to prevent Emerson from coming to the net and taking control of the action.

"If a server hits his first serve too long, his second one figures to be deep, where he wants it, because he only needs to ease up slightly and it's in," he explained in *Advantage Ashe*. "But if his first serve catches the net, his next ought to be juicy because he hasn't found the range. He's up against the old principle that it's harder to speed up than to slow down."

Ashe broke Emerson's serve in the very first game and took the opening set, 13–11. Then he held on for the second set as well, 6–4. Only one more set separated Ashe from his greatest victory so far.

But Emerson refused to be dispatched so easily. He battled back in the third set for a hard-fought 12–10 triumph and a chance to even up the match by taking the fourth set. Instead of panicking, Ashe remained calm, and his self-discipline paid off: He won the set handily, 6–2, and knocked out the tournament's defending champion. "For 24 hours I was a hero—the big hope to stop foreign domination of U.S. tennis," Ashe recalled. "The Richmond *News Leader* put the story of my upset win on its front page. And my father took the train up from Virginia to watch me play [Spain's Manuel] Santana in the semifinals."

Ashe's quest for the Forest Hills title ended quickly, in three sets, thanks to Santana's touch and artistry. Nevertheless, Ashe's confidence was sky high. "Naturally I hit the trail harder now," he said. "I was like a hunting dog that sniffs something good. Beating Emerson showed me that I might be able to lick anybody in the wide world."

Ashe took a giant step toward that end in the fall of 1965, when he traveled with the U.S. Davis Cup team to play a few exhibitions in New Zealand and then compete in Australia. After the young American team of Frank Froehling, Clark Graebner, and Dennis Ralston had lost to Spain in Barcelona, Coach McCall had decided that they needed to gain more international experience; he promptly planned a trip

Second Lieutenant Arthur Ashe in the military uniform he wore from 1966 to 1968 during his stint in the army. The black-rimmed eyeglasses had become a part of his look during his college years.

for them to the land down under, to enable Ashe and the others to go head-to-head with some of the world's top players. Ashe realized that the time away from school would push back his graduation to June but decided to join the team just the same. In Australia, where summer was just about to begin, he could brush up on his grass-court game—something he would have to wait half a year to do in the Northern Hemisphere.

Ashe had one other reason for making the trip: Helping the United States win the Davis Cup was his chief goal in tennis. "Tournaments are no sweat, but you lose sleep in the Davis Cup," he said. "If you lose a tournament, it's just *you* losing. If you lose in the Davis Cup, the United States has lost."

Electing to go on the trip proved to be one of Ashe's wisest decisions. Free to concentrate on nothing but tennis for three straight months, he proceeded to put on a formidable display. He won four tournaments—the first man to do so in Australia since Rod Laver in 1962—came in second in two others, and beat the highly vaunted Emerson twice. Harry Hopman, Australia's Davis Cup captain, said after watching his countrymen get torn apart by Ashe, "He is the most promising player in the world today and the single biggest threat to our Davis Cup supremacy."

Ashe would score one more important victory before he graduated from UCLA in the spring of 1966, but it was not on the tennis court. Richmond, the city that had prevented him from playing on many of its tennis courts because of his skin color, had decided to honor its now-famous native son. February 4, 1966, was declared Arthur Ashe Day.

Ashe was put up the night before the main festivities in the city's swankest hotel, the John Marshall, and attended a banquet on his behalf. He was honored the next day by members of the local legislature at City Hall, where the mayor and several of Ashe's close friends, including Ronald Charity and Dr. Robert Johnson, were featured speakers. When it was Ashe's turn to address the crowd, he told his listeners, "Ten years ago this would not have happened. It is as much a tribute to Richmond and the state of Virginia as it is to me."

That June, a week after he graduated from UCLA, Ashe reported to ROTC training camp at Fort Lewis, Washington, to fulfill his two-year obligation to the military. He was appointed to a position of responsibility, deputy brigade commander, but soon got

Ashe practices on the United States Military Academy's tennis courts in West Point, New York. "I have three different backhands," he said. "I can hit a flat backhand, on top of the ball or under it."

more than he bargained for. On his first day there, his immediate superior, the cadet brigade commander, sprained an ankle and had to be taken to the infirmary. Ashe, who had no experience leading men in military drills, suddenly found himself in charge of a unit of 800 soldiers. After that overwhelming assignment, the rest of his six weeks at Fort Lewis seemed relatively easy.

When boot camp ended in midsummer, Ashe was formally inducted into the army. A short time later, he ran into Bill Cullen, coach of the United States Military Academy's tennis team, at the Eastern Grass

Court Championships. Cullen invited him to become assistant coach at West Point, as the New York–based institution is informally known, and Ashe quickly accepted. He was elated to have the opportunity to continue working on his game while serving in the army. For good measure, Cullen combined Ashe's assistant coaching job with the untaxing position of data-processing officer.

Leading the life of both a second lieutenant and a tennis player proved difficult, however, and Ashe's game suffered a few noticeable lapses during the next two years. There were several high points—he made it to the U.S. Indoor Championship finals in 1966, won the U.S. Clay Court Championships in 1967, and ran his Davis Cup singles record at one point to 9–0—but his overall performance was not as impressive as he would have liked.

Seeded fifth at the 1966 U.S. Nationals, where he had previously made it to the finals, he lost in straight sets to John Newcombe of Australia in the third round. He suffered two embarrassing losses in 1967 Davis Cup action, falling to both Miguel Olvera and Pancho Guzman of lightly regarded Ecuador. Military obligations also caused him to miss several major tournaments, including Wimbledon in 1966 and 1967 and the U.S. National Championships in 1967.

All told, Ashe finished 1967 the same way he had ended 1966: as the nation's number two amateur player. In 1966, he had been ranked behind only Dennis Ralston; now his good friend Charlie Pasarell was the sole person ahead of him. Going into 1968, Ashe said, "I knew I would have to try harder."

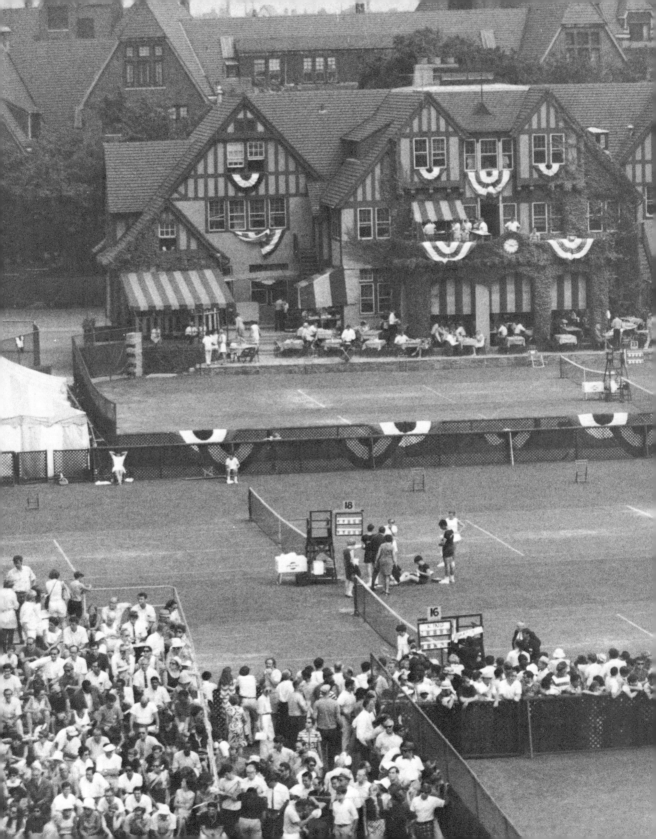

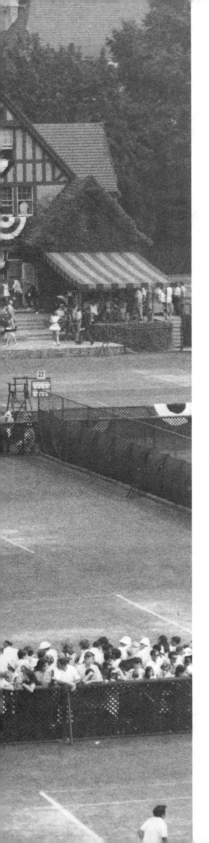

5

THE DREAM
COMES TRUE

ARTHUR ASHE HAD shown by 1968 that he
had more than enough talent to battle for the number
one spot in tennis. Anyone who had watched him
belt his incredibly hard topspin backhand or unleash
his devastating cannonball serve knew that he possessed the strokes to move up in the rankings. He
had certainly displayed signs that he was ready to do
so: He had scored impressive victories over some of
the game's leading players, had won a variety of tournaments, and had performed well as a member of the
U.S. Davis Cup team.

Yet Ashe had not captured any of the top championships—the Australian, French, U.S., or Wimbledon—the four tournaments that make up tennis's
Grand Slam. In addition, his Davis Cup heroics had
come in early rounds of the competition, before the
pressure was at its height. His fortunes would change
in 1968.

It all began for Ashe at Wimbledon in late June,
a time when the entire tennis world was undergoing
a revolution. Ever since the start of organized tennis,
professionals had been forbidden to compete against

---

*The U.S. Nationals, a tournament that was closed to profession-
als, was held at Forest Hills until 1968, when the open tennis era
began and the West Side Tennis Club became the home of the
U.S. Open. Ashe won both events that year—the only man ever
to achieve that distinction.*

amateurs. Accordingly, the most prestigious tournaments were traditionally reserved for amateurs such as Ashe while excluding Rod Laver and others as soon as they turned pro. This arrangement often prevented the public from watching the best players go up against one another.

In March 1968, after Roy Emerson, John Newcombe, Ken Rosewall, and other top players joined the professional ranks, the sport's governing body, the International Tennis Federation (ITF), finally gave its approval to open tennis. Professionals and amateurs alike thus became eligible to compete at a number of tournaments, including Wimbledon and the newly created U.S. Open. As a result, when Ashe went to Wimbledon in the summer of 1968, he squared off against the world's best.

Ashe came into the tournament as the 13th seed. He had been performing extremely well, especially in Davis Cup play, racking up six straight victories against the British Caribbean, Mexico, and Ecuador. (His matches against Lance Lumsden and Richard Russell of the British Caribbean took place at Byrd Park in Richmond, on the very same courts that had been denied to him by Jim Crow laws during his youth.)

Ashe was just as dominating in the early rounds at Wimbledon. He won straight set victories over Eduardo Zuleta, Ismail El Shafei, and Ove Bengtson. But in the fourth round, he was paired against John Newcombe, the reigning Wimbledon and U.S. Nationals champion. Although their playing styles were strikingly similar—both the 23-year-old Newcombe and the 24-year-old Ashe relied on a powerful serve-and-volley game—Newcombe appeared to hold a slight advantage over Ashe coming into the match. The tournament's fourth seed was a professional who devoted all his time to tennis, whereas Lieutenant Ashe was only a part-time player.

A powerful serve-and-volleyer, Australia's John Newcombe was one of the top players who stood in Ashe's path as the world's best black player made his way up the tennis ranks. "Newcombe distracts you and makes you think ahead, wondering what he is going to come up with next," Ashe said. "It's a great psychological trick, for you may do more damage to yourself worrying about when he is going to run around his backhand than when in fact he does it."

Ashe won the first two sets, 6–4 and 6–4, then Newcombe turned the match around. He took the third set convincingly, 6–1, and held on in the fourth set, 6–4. The momentum had clearly swung over to his side.

And yet the early action in the fifth set seemed to favor Ashe. He began the set by holding his serve easily, then he threatened to break Newcombe's serve. "If I lead when I'm receiving," he explained in *Advantage Ashe*, "I edge to my right and open up my backhand angle for the server. I have a high-octane backhand. I'm telling him, 'Hit it to my backhand and you'll get blasted as usual. Hit it to my forehand and you'll probably fault because it's such a narrow angle.' " In Newcombe's fourth service game of the set, Ashe's strategy of pressuring his opponent finally paid off. Ashe rifled a backhand down the line for a 5–3 advantage in the set, then held serve to win the match.

Ashe's victory over Newcombe advanced him into the quarterfinals against the Netherlands' Tom Okker, who was nicknamed the Flying Dutchman.

Ashe lost a tough opening set, 9–7, but continued to fight hard and took the next two sets by the same score, before finishing off Okker in the fourth set, 6–2.

Rod Laver, Ashe's next opponent, was not nearly as compliant. The deceptive left-hander rolled over Ashe, 7–5, 6–2, 6–4, in the semifinals on July 5 and won the tournament two days later. Nevertheless, Ashe had put on an impressive showing at Wimbledon—his best in four appearances.

The following month in Cleveland, Ohio, the U.S. Davis Cup team, with the help of two Ashe victories, defeated Spain in the first round of the interzone finals and won the right to play India in the second round. A week later, in mid-August, having posted 12 straight victories, he entered the U.S. National Championships at the Longwood Cricket Club in Brookline, Massachusetts, as the tournament's top seed. True to form, he won his first five matches and earned a berth in the finals. Only his Davis Cup teammate Bob Lutz stood between Ashe and the title.

The final was anything but a cakewalk for Ashe. The match took place on August 25 in 90-degree heat and lasted a total of 53 games. Lutz, who had beaten the highly regarded Clark Graebner in the previous round, took control of the action by eking out a 10–8 victory in the third set to gain a 2-sets-to-1 edge. Somehow, Ashe found a new sense of determination. He breezed through the next set, 6–0, and won the decisive fifth set, 6–4, for the championship. Winning the title established him as the top-ranked amateur in the United States.

Ashe braced himself for another mighty challenge the following week, when professionals and amateurs alike converged on Forest Hills for the first U.S. Open. Ashe had little trouble winning his first two matches, but his third-round opponent, Roy Emerson, was not to be taken lightly. "To beat him," Ashe said, "you've got to draw errors . . . mix up lots of garbage for him—spins, twists, lobs, now and then a straight hard drive to keep him guessing, then maybe a drop shot."

Ashe did just that. He toppled Emerson in straight sets to advance to the quarterfinals against South Africa's Cliff Drysdale. The tournament's fifth seed, Ashe dropped the first set to Drysdale, 10–8, then tore through him in three straight sets. Just as at Wimbledon, the previous Grand Slam event, Ashe had made it to the semifinals.

Ashe's opponent was a familiar foe: Davis Cup teammate Clark Graebner, whose strong, clean-cut features had earned him the nickname Superman. The first time Ashe and Graebner met, at the 1956 National Boys' Championships in Kalamazoo, they were both 13 years old. In the 12 years since then, they had played and practiced together all around the globe and had got to know each other extremely well. Neither man was looking forward to knocking his friend out of the tournament.

As in his quarterfinal match against Drysdale, Ashe started off slowly. He lost the first set, 6–4, and came within a point of losing his serve in the first game of the second set. But Graebner sliced a return of serve wide to bring the score to deuce, and then Ashe played two perfect points to hold serve.

After that, Ashe's play picked up considerably. With the score in his favor, 7–6, in the second set, he raced after a hard volley down the line and flicked a sharply angled backhand across the court, past an astonished Graebner; the shot landed on the line to create a set point for Ashe. He cashed in quickly, drawing Graebner to the net and then lobbing over him to capture the point and the set, 8–6.

Ashe continued to make exceptional shots throughout the next two sets and won them 7–5 and

6–2. Coming out on top in the match put him in a position to win the first Grand Slam event of his career. His opponent would be a man with revenge on his mind: Tom Okker.

The first set of the 1968 U.S. Open men's championship seemed to go on forever. Rain had caused the final to be delayed until September 9, and the extra day's wait appeared to have left both players a bit tense. They began by playing conservatively as they tried to feel out each other's game.

With the set dragging on for nearly half an hour, Ashe served two consecutive aces in the 11th game. (All told, he would rocket 15 serves past Okker, a phenomenal total, during the set.) Okker jokingly turned his back as if to surrender as Ashe prepared for his next serve. But subduing Okker was not that easy. Indeed, it was not until the 26th game that Ashe broke Okker's serve and won the set, 14–12.

Losing such a long, emotionally exhausting set should have left Okker demoralized. Yet he bounced right back. "Okker," according to Ashe, "has no nerves as we know them." Although he continued to have difficulty handling Ashe's powerful first serve, he looked to jump all over Ashe's slower second serve and met with some success. Okker took the second set, 7–5, to even up the match.

The next series of games repeated the patterns established in the first two sets. Ashe won the third set, 6–3, to take the lead; Okker came right back in the fourth set, 6–3, to tie the score at two sets apiece, with one more set still to be played.

"Nobody can imagine, unless they've been through it, what agony you face in a close five-set match, especially in scorching weather, and more especially in a late round of a top tournament," Ashe wrote in *Advantage Ashe*. "Your feet hurt, your racket hand hurts, your one-pound racket is as heavy as a shovel, maybe your head pounds and your eyes burn

Ashe with his father, who was on hand at the 1968 U.S. Open on September 9 to watch his son outlast Tom Okker in five sets, 14–12, 5–7, 6–3, 3–6, 6–3, to capture the men's singles title. "It's my national championship," Ashe said of the U.S. Open, "so I value it even higher than Wimbledon."

from the sun." Unlike most other sports, he noted, tennis does not allow you to "sit down and let a substitute go in for you. You can't even call time out."

Fortunately for Ashe, he was in the best shape of his life. He was a well-trained athlete, and the army put him through a tough regimen every day. As a result, he was physically *and* mentally stronger than he had ever been.

Ashe, who had not lost a match in 2 months— he had taken 25 in a row—felt supremely confident. "I went back to serve the first game of the final set," he recalled in *Off the Court,* "and everything seemed to be building. My father was in the stands. So was Dr. Johnson. It was the first U.S. Open." He would not let this chance slip by.

A great believer in community work, Ashe takes time out from his busy schedule to speak with a group of youngsters at a tennis clinic in Washington, D.C. According to Ashe, "At some point, you have to face up to your place in American society."

Ashe held serve in the opening game of the fifth set. With the score knotted at 30 in the following game, he placed a nifty lob just inches inside the baseline, well out of the rushing Okker's reach, to gain the advantage. Then he angled a crosscourt forehand on the next point to break Okker's serve and take a 2–0 lead.

Each player held serve twice to put the score at 4–2 in Ashe's favor. All he had to do now was hold his serve two more times. If he could manage that, the championship would be his.

Suddenly, Ashe's plans threatened to come apart. He found himself on the verge of losing his edge in the seventh game, when Okker jumped all over a second serve and passed him at the net to force a break point. Realizing that it was vital for him to win the next point, Ashe elected to serve to Okker's weaker side, the backhand. "I don't hammer a man's soft spot constantly, because he may strengthen it," he said in *Advantage Ashe*. "I just save it as a trump up my sleeve for moments when I really need a point. So if his backhand is shaky, I play mostly to his forehand. He thinks he's doing better than he is. When the time comes to knock him over, then I put pressure on his weakness." And that is exactly what Ashe did. He served three straight balls to Okker's backhand and won each point easily to capture the game.

The next time Ashe stepped to the service line, he was serving for the match. He opened the game by volleying a forehand beyond Okker's reach. Then Ashe served an ace to take a 30–love lead. Next, he forced Okker to miss a backhand. Now ahead 40–love, Ashe cranked up a powerful serve, rushed the net to retrieve Okker's return, and punched a volley past him for the final winner of the day.

Ashe immediately spun around and pointed his racket at the stadium wall as though he were spraying gunfire. The West Point lieutenant had shot down every challenger and now stood alone. He raised his arms over his head, his fists clasped together in victory. Arthur Ashe, Sr., rushed down from his seat in the stands and cried with delight when he came onto the court. "Well done, son," he said. The two Ashes hugged each other in joy.

Being the first black male to win a Grand Slam tournament thrust Ashe into the public eye as never before. He was besieged by interviewers and honored everywhere he went. Perhaps his most satisfying moment took place upon his return to West Point. When he walked into the mess hall to dine with the cadets, they greeted him with a thunderous standing ovation.

Ashe took all the fuss in stride. "It's nice to hear the announcer say, 'Point . . . Ashe,' " he told the

Ashe finally lays his hands on the trophy he has been coveting more than any other after the United States defeated Australia, four matches to one, in the final round of the 1968 Davis Cup. Joining him in the victory celebration are U.S. captain Donald Dell (center) and teammate Clark Graebner.

press shortly after he won the U.S. Open, "but I'd rather hear him say, 'Point . . . United States.' " He soon got his wish. In early November, the U.S. Davis Cup team met India in Puerto Rico. Ashe defeated both Premjit Lall and Ramanathan Krishnan to lead the U.S. squad into the Cup finals against the Aussies in Adelaide, Australia.

For the first time in many years, the U.S. team was not an underdog against the Aussies. Not only was Ashe playing better than anyone in the world, but the Australian team was missing its big guns— Emerson, Laver, Newcombe, and Rosewall—who were all professionals and therefore ineligible for Davis Cup competition. Instead of them, Captain Harry Hopman had to count on Bill Bowrey, Australia's national amateur champion; left-hander Ray Ruffels; and 17-year-old John Alexander. No player on either side had ever been in a Davis Cup final, however. "Sure, we're the favorites," said U.S. captain Donald Dell, "and we should be. But coming down to Australia to play against Australians under Harry Hopman is a tough proposition."

Graebner won the opening match against Bowrey on December 26 to give the U.S. a 1–0 lead, and Ashe, after a slow start, won his match against Ruffels in four sets. On the following day, the U.S. doubles team of Stan Smith and Bob Lutz took the court against Ruffels and Alexander. A victory by the U.S. pair would bring home the Cup.

Ashe and Graebner were too nervous to watch the match. They got into a car and drove around Adelaide, tuning in to the contest on the radio. Smith and Lutz took the first two sets handily. Then, with the U.S. twosome leading 5–2, Ashe listened intently as the announcer called the final points of the match. "The dream had come true" was Ashe's immediate response. "All the hours and days of travel, practice, strange hotel rooms, foreign accents, aching shins and elbows had converged on this point in time. It was worth it. We had won the Davis Cup." ❧

6

COURTING FAME

THE TRIUMPHANT U.S. Davis Cup team passed through Southeast Asia on its way back from Australia in early 1969, making stops in Burma, Cambodia, Hong Kong, Indonesia, Japan, Laos, Thailand, Vietnam, and the Philippines. There they visited hospitals and U.S. military installations and held tennis exhibitions to entertain the American troops stationed overseas to fight in the Vietnam War. The players, hailed as national heroes, were feted by generals and ambassadors. They were even invited to the White House to visit with President Lyndon B. Johnson.

None of the players attracted more notice than 25-year-old Arthur Ashe. He had always drawn his fair share of media attention by being the only black star in the tennis world. But when his Davis Cup and U.S. Open victories in 1968 resulted in his being ranked the number one player in America, his fame skyrocketed in a way he never could have predicted.

Ashe became a very hot property. His image graced the covers of *Life* magazine and *Sports Illustrated*, and a long profile on him appeared in the *New Yorker*. With the help of his adviser, Donald Dell, he negotiated contracts with Head, a maker of sporting goods, to have them sell a racket with his name on it, the Arthur Ashe Competition, and with Cat-

From the mid-1960s on, Ashe took an increasingly active role in campaigning for black rights. "Prominent black athletes have a responsibility to champion the causes of their race," he told a panel on the television program "Face the Nation" in 1969.

73

Ashe's toughest opponent over the years was Australia's Rod Laver, nicknamed the Rocket because he was capable of blasting a point-winner from any spot on the court, particularly at the net. "His volleys," Ashe observed, "come back like lightning."

alina to promote its line of tennis wear. He also signed on as a spokesman for Philip Morris, put on tennis clinics for Coca-Cola and American Express, and became tennis director at the Doral Country Club in Miami, Florida. His success on the tennis court was proving to pay huge financial dividends.

Ashe's shift in fortunes was accompanied by a change in life-style. He moved to a swank apartment on New York City's Upper East Side and became known as one of the nation's most eligible young men. When he went out on dates with singer Diana Ross and top fashion model Beverly Johnson, his activities were documented in the tabloids.

In part because of the distractions that came with his success—a sore elbow, which forced him to miss several tournaments, did not help matters—Ashe failed to post the same kind of results in 1969 that he had achieved the previous year. Whereas he won 10 tournaments in 1968, he managed to win only 2 in 1969. The highlight of the year was undoubtedly his 6–2, 15–13, 7–5 win over Romania's Ilie Nastase in the first match of the Davis Cup finals. Ashe's victory on September 19 set the tone for his teammates. They blanked the Romanians, 5–0, to win their second straight Cup.

Ashe enjoyed several other shining moments in 1969. He made it again to the Wimbledon semifinals—beating his childhood hero, Pancho Gonzales, along the way—before being eliminated by Rod Laver in four sets. Ashe also reached the semifinals at the U.S. Open, only to have Laver knock him out again, this time needing only three sets to accomplish the feat. (Ashe always had trouble beating "the Rocket," who captured his second career Grand Slam in 1969; his overall match record against the left-hander was 3–22.)

Off the court, Ashe made several winning moves. During the summer of 1969, World Championship Tennis (WCT), an organization that staged tournaments around the globe, offered him a five-year contract to compete in its events. Ashe chose to remain his own boss. "I value my independence too much to be told where and when I have to play," he said the following January.

Eager to sign America's top player, WCT eased its demands and offered Ashe a contract with many fewer restrictions. Upon agreeing to its terms, he saw the balance in his bank account increase considerably from two years earlier. When he had won the U.S. Open in 1968, he had to forgo the $14,000 earmarked for him because he was still an amateur and therefore ineligible to receive any prize money. (To console Ashe, an anonymous admirer had sent him a gift of stock that was worth $8,900.) Now, in 1970, he was to receive about $50,000 from WCT as a first-year pro.

Even though Ashe and a number of other players were earning a hefty amount of money, they felt that they were not getting their fair share. Tennis had been growing in popularity by leaps and bounds during the late 1960s and early 1970s: Tournaments were drawing more fans, and televised matches were garnering larger audiences. The sport thus became very profitable for the people who brought the matches to the public. But the amount of prize money offered to the players did not rise proportionately.

Ashe took part in a dignified campaign to improve the players' plight. Without ever coming off as greedy or selfish, he and several others had formed the International Tennis Players Association (ITPA) in 1969—Ashe acted as treasurer—to protect their interests. The ITPA evolved into the Association of Tennis Professionals in 1972, with Ashe serving as the union's vice-president.

The ATP did not waste much time in making its presence felt. Ashe helped the association organize a boycott of Wimbledon in 1973, with its members refusing to play in the tournament because Nikki Pilic of Yugoslavia had been banned from all International Tennis Federation events, including Wimbledon, for failing to uphold a promise he had made to play on the Yugoslavian Davis Cup team. The ATP refused to have its members bullied. As Ashe put it, "If Nikki Pilic could be forced to play Davis Cup and denied entry to Wimbledon, then wouldn't a precedent be set where, say, I would be forced to play some rinky-dink tournament at the risk of being denied admittance to Forest Hills?"

On the night of June 19, less than a week before the start of Wimbledon, Ashe and his fellow executive officers of the ATP voted to have the association's members withdraw from the tournament. Their proposal was put before the full ATP membership the following morning, and hardly anyone objected to skipping the event. "There is still a Wimbledon left for 1973," Ashe said at the time, "but it is not the championship of the world." When the various parties finally worked out a compromise months later, Ashe and his peers had gained greater freedom in shaping their tennis schedule.

Ashe's activism was not limited to the world of tennis. In 1969, he applied for a visa to South Africa to play tennis there. Cliff Drysdale, who had left his native country in protest of its policies of racial segregation and political and economic discrimination against its black population, had warned Ashe that the South African government would never let him in. Drysdale was right; Ashe's visa application was turned down.

That July, Ashe decided to take a stand. "This time I won't be silent," he said at a press conference. "I'll go right to the South African embassy in New York. If they want to turn me down, they'll have to do it right there in front of all of you." Eager to make sure that the entire world knew about his problem, Ashe enlisted the support of U.S. secretary of state William Rogers, the United States Lawn Tennis Association, the South African Lawn Tennis Union, and several South African players. He made a statement that he wanted to visit South Africa to "play tennis and only play tennis," but the nation still denied his visa request. "Ashe's general antagonism toward South Africa's racial policies" was the reason, a government official said. A visit by him might incite violence.

Ashe countered quickly. He called for expelling South Africa from the ITF and asked that the country be banned from Davis Cup competition. Backed by a wide range of supporters from around the world,

Ashe won this battle. South Africa was expelled from Davis Cup competition in February 1970.

Although Ashe limited his crusade against South Africa to its participation in international tennis, he played a key role in bringing its oppressive system of apartheid to the world's attention. The U.S. government, recognizing Ashe's concern about South Africa, invited him to speak before the African subcommittee of the House of Representatives Foreign Relations Committee in Washington, D.C. Ashe supported a host of measures to pressure South Africa to reform but told the committee he did not endorse banning South African athletes from playing in America. Ashe wanted to punish the government, not the individuals who did not have a role in shaping the country's discriminatory policies. "My moral conscience tells me we should not stoop to the level of South Africa," he explained.

In 1970, the U.S. government also invited Ashe to serve as a goodwill ambassador. Both he and Stan Smith, America's number one player at the time (Ashe had dropped to number two), were asked by the U.S. State Department to tour Africa. The two traveled to Kenya, Nigeria, Tanzania, and Uganda and met with heads of state, university students, and ambassadors, just like on Ashe's trip to Southeast Asia with the Davis Cup team the previous year.

Ashe returned to Africa for three weeks in 1971 to tour Cameroon, Gabon, Senegal, and the Ivory Coast with Tom Okker, Charlie Pasarell, and Marty Riessen. At a tennis club in Cameroon, he spotted a youngster who showed a remarkable amount of athletic ability. The boy's name was Yannick Noah.

Ashe arranged to send Noah to France, where Philippe Chatrier, president of the French Tennis Federation, took one look at the youth's game and decided he was a budding star. Both Ashe and Chatrier proved to be good judges of talent. At the age

As part of his world tennis tour, Ashe competed in tournaments at various exotic locations, including the South Vietnamese city of Saigon. "Playing the tour," he said, "is much different from being on a team. You must depend more on yourself, of course; and you must depend on the people you beat for friendship."

of 20, Noah emerged as the number one player in France.

Back in America, Ashe continued to apply for a visa to South Africa, but each request was denied. Then, in 1973, his visa was approved. The South African government wanted its athletes to take part in the 1976 Olympic Games and realized it would have to make some concessions in its international policy in order to participate.

Ashe was surprised by this change in circumstance, but he did not stop there. As soon as he had won this opening, he pressed for more. He laid down three conditions for his visit: He would not play before a racially segregated audience; he refused to be made an "honorary white," as had been asked of other blacks traveling in South Africa; and he requested that he be allowed to go wherever he pleased and say whatever he wanted. The government agreed to all three of his demands.

Ashe's proposed trip immediately became a source of controversy among many blacks in the United States and South Africa. Some of them felt that he was playing into the South African government's hands by going there: The government would claim that its system of apartheid was not so terrible if people such as Ashe were willing to visit the country. Others criticized him for paying so much attention to the plight of blacks in Africa while there were so many unresolved racial problems in America. Similarly, when he had discovered Yannick Noah in Africa, some people had claimed that Ashe should spend more time helping black Americans develop into tennis players and worry less about those in Africa.

"My own case is complicated by the fact that I'm the only one," Ashe said at the time. "I am *the* black tennis player, a bloc by myself." As he noted later, "The predicament I'm in is that if I don't spread out my assistance, people become upset: I become the bad guy and I can't win."

Nevertheless, Ashe enjoyed his share of significant victories, with one of the biggest occurring during his initial trip to South Africa. When he played in the South African Open in November 1973, it marked the first time in the country's history that a black competed in the event.

The blacks who came to Johannesburg's Ellis Park rooted enthusiastically for Ashe, who played well in the tourney. He made it to the finals, winning 12 sets in a row before losing the singles title to Jimmy Connors in straight sets. Then he teamed up with Tom Okker to win the doubles competition. "In a way, this might have been the most important doubles match I ever won," he noted in *Arthur Ashe: Portrait in Motion*, "for now a black's name rests on the list of South African tennis champions. Etched. Forever."

For the most part, though, Ashe's name did not appear on the champions board during the early 1970s as frequently as it did during the 1960s. The lone exception was in 1970, when he came back strong from his disappointing 1969 season and played almost as well as he had in 1968. Ashe competed in 30 tournaments in 1970 and came out on top in 11 of them while reaching the finals in 3 others. Overall, he won 91 matches against only 20 defeats. His biggest win of the year was the Australian Open, one of the sport's four major tournaments. He had made it to the finals of the Australian Open twice before, in 1966 and 1967, but had lost each time to Roy Emerson. Ashe finally got over the hump in 1970 by beating Richard Crealy in straight sets, 6–4, 9–7, 6–2.

Ashe played in 123 tournaments from 1971 through 1974 and won only 11 of them. His winning percentage, which in 1968 had reached a high of 88 percent of the matches he played and was close to 80 percent in 1970, dropped dramatically, to near 70 percent from 1971 through 1973. He turned things around a bit in 1974, taking 76 percent of his matches and reaching the finals in 11 tournaments, but it was not easy.

Old pros such as Emerson, Laver, Tony Roche, and Ken Rosewall were still playing solid tennis. The best players from Ashe's own generation, which included Nastase, Smith, and John Newcombe, now had several years on the tour under their belt and were playing exceptionally well. In addition, a new crop of talented young performers was beginning to assert itself; chief among these players were Bjorn Borg, Jimmy Connors, and Guillermo Vilas.

With so much top-level competition around, the media began to suggest that Ashe was spending too much of his time attending to business matters and running the ATP, of which he had become president, and was neglecting his game. Ashe, however, was not yet ready to view himself as the tennis world was starting to: as a great player who, at the age of 31, had passed his peak. 🌸

An American star in stripes: At the request of the U.S. State Department, Ashe visited several African nations as a goodwill ambassador in 1970. He made another important trip to the Dark Continent three years later, when he became the first black to compete in the South African Open.

7

GLORY AGAIN!

Ashe holds up a check for $50,000, part of his reward for winning the 1975 World Championship Tennis (WCT) finals on May 11 in Dallas, Texas. The WCT tournament was his first significant singles title in five years; less than two months later, though, he would walk away with an even more important championship: the men's title at Wimbledon.

AFTER SEVERAL YEARS of subpar play, Arthur Ashe knew his tennis career was at a crossroads as the 1975 season began. Even though he had triumphed in 11 tournaments over the last 4 years, he had not won a major singles event since 1970, when he captured the Australian Open. He had, in fact, shown several signs of regaining his old form in 1974, making it to the finals in 11 different tourneys. Yet he won only two of them.

Tennis experts began to say that the 31-year-old Ashe was no longer able to win the big matches. He was being beaten at his own game of serve-and-volley tennis by the likes of John Newcombe and Roscoe Tanner, and he was not faring much better against the new generation of talented players who had developed a style to counter the serve-and-volleyers. Rising stars such as Bjorn Borg and Jimmy Connors could hit extremely hard and precise passing shots; they practically dared their opponents to come to the net because they were so confident they could pass them.

Ashe, ranked fifth in the United States, was not about to drop further in the rankings without a fight. He set two ambitious goals for himself in 1975. First, he hoped to capture the WCT Championships, held that spring in Dallas. He also wanted to win Wimbledon. He had made it to the All-England semifinals twice before but had been beaten both times. To make a last stand would require some tactical changes, though.

Ashe recognized that the leading players on the tour could not be outslugged; they had to be outsmarted. Accordingly, he mixed in some dinks and chip shots with his already wide array of strokes and began to play like a wily veteran.

But that was not all he did. Ashe also realized that at his age he could not depend solely on playing in tournaments to keep himself in top condition. If he wanted to feel strong at the end of a grueling match against a younger opponent, he had to pound his body into better shape. Over the past few years, it seemed that he was constantly having to come back from nagging injuries. The time had come to put a stop to them.

Ashe recalled how a rigorous weight-training regimen at West Point in 1967 had helped prepare him for his great year in 1968. He decided to undergo a similar program in early 1975. Accompanied by Henry Hines, a world-class long jumper who acted as his conditioning coach, he flew to Puerto Rico to train for the upcoming year.

Ashe's off-season training paid immediate dividends. Even though he was suffering from a slight injury to his left heel, he defeated Bjorn Borg on May 11 to win the finals of the WCT Championships. First prize included a solid-gold tennis ball worth more than $33,000 at the time.

Winning the WCT title caused Ashe's confidence to soar higher than it had been in years. He decided to skip the French Open and most other clay-court events that spring and devote himself to England's grass-court circuit as a way of preparing for Wimbledon. He won a tournament in Beckenham and per-

Among the first of tennis's new breed of young stars, Sweden's Bjorn Borg was primarily a baseline player known for his powerful ground strokes and intense concentration. Ashe knocked him out of both the WCT Championship finals and Wimbledon quarterfinals in 1975, just a year before Borg began his rise to the top of men's tennis by winning the first of five consecutive Wimbledon titles.

formed well at Nottingham before losing a tough match to Tony Roche. By the time Wimbledon began on June 23, he felt in fine form.

The sixth seed at Wimbledon, Ashe buzzed through his first two matches, beating Bob Hewitt, 7–5, 3–6, 6–2, 6–4, and then whipping Japan's Jun Kamiwazumi in straight sets, 6–2, 7–5, 6–4. Next, he trounced fellow American Brian Gottfried, a solid player, 6–2, 6–3, 6–1. Great Britain's Graham Stilwell, who had upset 10th-seeded John Alexander, fell to Ashe in the fourth round, 6–2, 5–7, 6–4, 6–2. He was now one of only eight players left in the draw.

Ashe's opponent in the quarterfinals was 19-year-old Bjorn Borg. The following year would see the young Swede win the first of an unprecedented five straight Wimbledon titles. But in 1975, Borg was not yet completely comfortable playing on grass, and he lost to Ashe, 2–6, 6–4, 8–6, 6–1, after taking the first set and leading 3–0 in the second.

In the semifinals, Ashe faced Tony Roche, who had defeated him only a few weeks earlier at Nottingham. Roche was playing extremely well, as his victories over Ken Rosewall and Tom Okker in his previous rounds attested. Yet Ashe prevailed in five tough sets, 5–7, 6–4, 7–5, 8–9, 6–4, to set up a showdown against the red-hot Jimmy Connors. The brash young American had won 96 percent of his matches in 1974 and was looking to improve upon that record in 1975. Yet Ashe dominated Connors in four sets, a feat that stunned the Centre Court crowd.

Without a doubt, Ashe's triumph at Wimbledon was the highlight of his year and among the shining moments of his career. And yet it was just one of many successes in 1975. All told, he played in 29 tournaments that year and made it to the finals in almost half of them, winning 9 and finishing as the runner-up in 5 others. He also competed for the U.S. Davis Cup team for the first time since 1970, beating Richard Russell of the British West Indies in his only Cup match that year.

Ashe's overall record for 1975 was 108 victories and 23 losses, which yielded the second-highest winning percentage (82 percent) of his career. Most important, though, it put the former army lieutenant on top of the tennis world. Not only did Ashe's U.S. ranking return to number one after a six-year hiatus, but in 1975 he attained, for the first time ever, the distinction of being ranked the top player in the world.

That year was not exactly Ashe's last hurrah— he won five more tournaments in 1976 and another three in 1978—but he never reached the same level of play again. Looking back on his career, he would trace the beginning of his decline to a loss in the 1976 WCT Championships in Dallas to Harold Solomon. An avowed baseliner who tried to beat his opponents by playing steady, fundamental tennis and outlasting them, Solomon ordinarily had difficulty beating someone like Ashe, who possessed a great variety of strokes. "I would not admit it then, but that loss marked the beginning of the end," Ashe said years later. "It was a signal, which I tried hard to ignore, that I had passed my peak as an athlete."

A few months later at Wimbledon, the signs began to point out even more clearly that Ashe's best tennis was behind him. Another American youth, Vitas Gerulaitis, beat Ashe, the tournament's second seed, in the fourth round. "Vitas was simply younger and faster," Ashe explained.

Luckily for Ashe, just as he was losing a step or two on the court, his personal life was falling perfectly into place. The first time he saw Jeanne Marie Moutoussamy was in New York City in October 1976, when she was taking his picture. A professional photographer, she was working at Madison Square Garden's Felt Forum, where a tennis tournament was being held to benefit the United Negro College Fund. Later in the day, at a reception after the tournament, Ashe asked her out. By their second date, he had a strong sense that their budding romance would blossom into marriage.

Nevertheless, it was difficult for Ashe to keep up a steady relationship; he was constantly on the go, traveling 11 months out of the year. When he went to Europe and then Australia in late 1976, he called her every day. Persistent problems with his heel caused him to return to New York in early 1977, much sooner than he had planned. Upon his arrival, he "made two decisions," he recalled in *Off the Court*: "I would have heel surgery and get married."

Ashe married Jeanne Marie Moutoussamy (second from left) on February 20, 1977, at the United Nations Chapel in New York City, with the Reverend Andrew Young (right), then the U.S. ambassador to the United Nations, performing the service. Because Ashe had bone chips removed from his heel 10 days before the wedding, he had to attend the ceremony with his left leg in a cast.

Wishing to surprise Jeanne with his proposal of marriage, Ashe placed an engagement ring in an envelope and put it in her medicine cabinet. It took her three days to find the ring, but when she did, she happily accepted his proposal. The two of them were married by his friend the Reverend Andrew Young, then the U.S. ambassador to the United Nations, on February 20, just 10 days after Ashe had bone chips removed from his heel. As a result of the operation, he had to hobble down the aisle at his wedding in a cast.

Although Ashe recovered quickly from the surgery, he did not remain injury free for very long. He hurt his foot in practice and decided to take the rest of 1977 off, skipping both Wimbledon and the U.S.

Open. With Ashe staying away from the circuit and his ranking beginning to decline, Catalina, the sportswear company he had been representing for the past eight years, decided to sever their business relationship. The company's decision was very painful for Ashe, who had helped build up Catalina's image only to be dropped by them.

Instead of being discouraged by such matters, Ashe simply worked hard to turn his fortunes around. He began to look for other business involvements in order to prepare for his life after tennis. He signed on with *Tennis* magazine to write a series of instructional articles for them, made television commercials for the National Guard, and took on other assignments. George Steinbrenner, in his fourth year as owner of the New York Yankees, offered him a front-office job with the ball club, but Ashe, an avowed baseball lover, turned the position down. His playing career was not yet over.

Ashe returned to the courts in early 1978 and won a $50,000 tournament in San Jose, California. Three months later, in Columbus, Ohio, he beat Bob Lutz in the finals of a $75,000 event. A short time after that, Ashe won what would prove to be the last title of his career, beating Brian Gottfried in Los Angeles to take the Pacific Southwest Championships.

This victory gave Ashe a shot at qualifying for the Grand Prix Masters in early 1979 at Madison Square Garden. (Regarded as the world series of tennis, this elite tournament features only the top eight players in the world.) Ashe convinced the management of the Doral Country Club in Miami, to whom he was still under contract, to let him bend the terms of their contract by permitting him to fly to Australia over the Christmas holidays. A good showing in the Australian Open would enable him to qualify for the Grand Prix Masters.

Hoping for a last hurrah in a tournament that featured the world's top male players, Ashe raises his arms in triumph on January 13 after earning a berth in the finals of the 1979 Grand Prix Masters at New York City's Madison Square Garden. A win over cofinalist John McEnroe would have provided a sweet ending for Ashe, whose playing career came to an end six months later, but he was unable to pull off the upset.

Before Ashe headed to Australia, though, he went to Sweden to compete in the interzone finals for the U.S. Davis Cup team. Ashe lost the opening match to Bjorn Borg in three sets but bounced back to beat Kjell Johansson in straight sets to advance the U.S. team into the final round. Ashe's success over Johansson was his 27th singles victory for the U.S. team, an American record for a Davis Cup player.

From Sweden, Ashe made the long trek to Australia, where he reached the semifinals of the Australian Open and thereby earned a berth in the Grand

Prix Masters. For a while, it looked as though the 35-year-old Ashe would pull off yet another stunning triumph. He began the tournament by besting both Brian Gottfried and Harold Solomon. When Jimmy Connors defaulted because of an injury, Ashe moved into the finals. There his opponent was an almost 20-year-old John McEnroe, who won the first of 3 consecutive U.S. Open titles later in the year. Ashe engineered two match points but could not convert either of them and wound up losing the Grand Prix Masters to McEnroe.

All told, Ashe competed in a total of 13 tournaments in 1979. He reached the finals in two of them, the U.S. Pro Indoor and the U.S. Indoor, but he came out second best in each. It would have provided a storybook ending to his illustrious career if he had managed to win one last contest before retiring from the circuit. In the middle of 1979, however, he found himself fighting for something far more urgent than a tennis trophy. ❦

8

"A NEW SEASON"

A POWERFUL PAIN in his chest awoke Arthur Ashe early in the night of July 30, 1979. He had just returned home to New York after having spent the past month competing at Wimbledon, where he was eliminated in the first round; vacationing in the south of France with his wife; and playing in a tennis exhibition at Kitzbühel, Austria. "The pain jolted me out of bed," he recalled in *Off the Court*. "While standing, I noticed that the two little fingers on both hands felt 'funny,' as if they had gone to sleep."

These sensations disappeared as suddenly as they came, and Ashe went back to bed. Then the pain and numbness recurred 15 minutes later. "I climbed out of bed, sweating," he remembered, "and walked around, bent over and clutching my chest." When the pain stopped once again, he went back to sleep. Forty-five minutes later, it struck for a third time.

The following morning, Ashe conducted a tennis clinic with Vitas Gerulaitis in the Bronx, then went to another clinic in the afternoon, at the East River Tennis Club in Long Island City. It was a scorching hot and muggy day. After signing autographs for some of his fans, Ashe suddenly found himself doubled over by a stabbing pain. As he had done the previous night, he tried to ignore the discomfort and waited for the terrible sensation to go away. This time it did not stop.

Ashe reveals the scar and suture marks left on his chest one week after successfully undergoing quadruple heart bypass surgery. The operation was performed on the 36-year-old tennis player in December 1979 to alleviate a life-threatening condition that was detected after he suffered a heart attack.

A doctor at the scene persuaded Ashe to go with him immediately to New York Hospital. "I want Mr. Ashe admitted very quickly as a heart attack patient," the physician told a nurse as soon as they entered the building.

Ashe was shocked by the doctor's words. A professional athlete in great physical shape, he found it hard to believe that at age 36 he had suffered a heart attack, even though his father had already experienced 2 of them and his mother had died during pregnancy of toxemia, which is caused in part by the same kinds of cardiovascular problems that lead to a heart attack. Ashe spent the next three days in the hospital, and his tests confirmed that he had indeed suffered an attack. Several of his coronary arteries were blocked, thereby straining his heart as it worked to pump blood throughout his body.

Subsequent tests prompted Ashe's physicians to tell him he would be severely handicapped by his condition for the rest of his life and would never play tennis again unless he underwent open-heart surgery. Later that summer, Ashe decided to undergo the operation. He checked into St. Luke's Hospital in December for a coronary bypass. In this procedure, one or more veins—four, in Ashe's case—are removed from another part of the patient's body, usually from the leg, and are joined to the obstructed arteries leading away from the heart. The newly planted veins give the blood a new, unblocked path through which to flow and thus ease the strain on the heart.

"The two greatest moments in my life were the day I married Jeannie and the morning I woke up alive: after surgery," Ashe said in 1980. Undergoing the bypass operation gave him the opportunity to lead a normal life once again. "I think you'll see me playing Wimbledon in June," he boldly predicted a week after the surgery. Ashe figured that he had been able to play well for many years in spite of suffering from cardiovascular disease. Now that the problem had been taken care of, he expected to feel in peak condition in a matter of months.

Ashe was overly optimistic, as it turned out. He underwent a battery of tests after being released from the hospital to see how his body would perform under stress, and the results were not very comforting. Then he went out for a run in early March and felt an intense pain in his chest; he realized that his body was not responding as he had hoped it would. His friend Dr. Doug Stein promptly asked Ashe to do a few jumping jacks. When the pain returned right away, Ashe finally understood that his body was telling him he could never play competitive tennis again. He called for a press conference on April 16, 1980, and publicly announced his retirement. He said he would "begin a new season of writing, talking, listening, and assisting."

Because Ashe's tennis career was beginning to wind down when his doctors detected his heart condition, making the adjustment from the life of a professional athlete to that of a former player was much easier than if he had been struck by cardiovascular disease years earlier. He had already made plans for how he would spend his time after he retired. Now he could follow up on them.

Still, Ashe did not have to give up tennis completely. In excellent health except for his heart condition, he could continue to play the sport, although only on a recreational basis. (He has to make sure he takes medication and monitors himself constantly when he undertakes any strenuous physical activity, including tennis. He also has to be very careful of his diet and must stay away from foods that are high in cholesterol, a fatlike substance that can block the veins and arteries.)

Ashe remained involved in competitive tennis by succeeding Tony Trabert as captain of the U.S. Davis

Cup team in 1981. Because Ashe always held the Davis Cup in high regard, the position meant a great deal to him. Three years earlier, in an article he had written for *World Tennis* magazine, he had attempted to explain its special hold on him.

> The Davis Cup endures as few other . . . institutions have done before it. The Davis Cup is not a place or a player, a cup or a contest, a name or a notion. It is an *idea*, and it will always be just that. Furthermore, it is not an accident that the word *ideal* is derived from the word *idea*. Dwight Davis must have been an idealist when in 1900 he went to the trouble of donating the huge silver bowl, a symbol of friendly tennis rivalry.
>
> Players who have played Davis Cup frequently, have gone to war against one another later, only to return after the wars are over to play again. Some have seen their countries conquer and be conquered, and the names of countries changed. The Davis Cup rules have changed, political systems have changed, even the cup itself has changed, but the idea and its ideals are immutable. The court is always 78 feet by 36 feet, and the highest standards of sportsmanship are demanded within those lines. Few countries can measure up to these ideals.

As much as Ashe upheld these ideals, not every player he coached on the U.S. team felt the same way. Most notable among them was young John McEnroe, with whom Ashe wound up having a stormy relationship. Like Ashe, McEnroe, who was recognized as the best player in the world, held the Davis Cup in great esteem. He was always quick to volunteer his services to the U.S. team, no matter how crowded his schedule was. Yet when he was on the court for a Davis Cup match, his behavior was often abusive.

As a result, the gentlemanly Ashe and the tempestuous McEnroe did not get along very well. To Ashe, the Davis Cup was tennis at its best, a team event that stressed a person's eagerness to play for his country and minimized his individual accomplish-

ments while bringing together players from various nations and helping them to establish friendly bonds. (He had forged especially close ties with many of the Australian players during the 1960s.) McEnroe's enthusiasm for Davis Cup play managed to increase public interest in the event. But his occasional outbursts directed at the linesmen and other officials were another matter.

Never were the differences between Ashe and McEnroe brought into clearer focus than at the 1981 Davis Cup semifinals against Australia. At a dinner prior to the matches, which were held in Portland,

Ashe, in his first year as captain of the U.S. Davis Cup team, confers with America's top player, John McEnroe, during the 1981 quarterfinals against Czechoslovakia. McEnroe's periodic outbursts of abusive language during match play ultimately strained his relationship with the gentlemanly Ashe.

Oregon, Ashe gave a speech on the importance of the Davis Cup. He told of the great friendships he had made and of the wonderful rivalries that had been established. The more he spoke about those fun-filled days, the more nostalgic he became. All at once, the usually cool Ashe became choked with emotion. When he tried to resume his speech moments later, he could not help himself: He broke into tears once again.

Within days of Ashe's speech, McEnroe and his doubles partner, Peter Fleming, took the court against Phil Dent and Peter McNamara in a match that could clinch the round for the Americans. Both U.S. players behaved badly throughout the course of the action, arguing with and berating the linesmen and the umpire. During one heated encounter with an official, play was delayed for five minutes. The American team ultimately received two formal warnings for conduct violation from the referee; a third warning would have meant instant disqualification. Dent, for one, called the Americans' display a "pretty poor show."

To Ashe, the pair's behavior was unacceptable. The Davis Cup captain told both McEnroe and Fleming that he would sooner pull them off the court and forfeit the match than watch them embarrass the United States with their unsportsmanlike behavior. Ashe apologized to the Australian team for his players' actions and went so far as to publicly call McEnroe's behavior "disgraceful."

McEnroe resented the criticism. He felt it was Ashe's role as captain to support his players, not chastise them. Even though he continued to play under Ashe through 1984, with the United States winning the Davis Cup in 1981 and 1982, McEnroe refused to forget Ashe's comments. After this incident, he reportedly agreed to remain on the U.S. team only if Ashe refrained from offering him any coaching advice.

If dealing with one difficult personality on the U.S. squad posed a problem for Ashe, dealing with two proved to be nearly impossible. In 1984, Jimmy Connors finally decided to volunteer his full services to the team. Up until that point, his Davis Cup career had been extremely brief; he had appeared in two rounds of play in 1976 and one round in 1981. Now, at age 32, he wanted to become an integral part of America's effort to recapture the Cup.

What a team his arrival made! The United States now had Connors and McEnroe, the two top American players, manning the court in the singles matches, and McEnroe and Fleming, yet to be defeated as a Davis Cup tandem, in the doubles competition. The U.S. squad appeared to be unbeatable.

But there were warring personalities for Ashe to contend with, and all of the bickering and infighting eventually took its toll. In addition to Ashe's failure to get along with either Connors or McEnroe, these two players disliked each other intensely and made the other team members feel ill at ease. The U.S. squad managed to vanquish Romania, Argentina, and Australia to make it to the Davis Cup finals against Sweden in December, but by then the Americans were ready to unravel. To one observer, Ashe was "quite unable to exert any authority over two millionaire superstars who would have no compunction in threatening to walk off the team if Ashe started to lay down the law." Connors had proved especially hard to handle. Whenever he was not playing, he left the arena rather than remain on the bench to cheer on his teammates.

Confident of their chances against Mats Wilander, Henrik Sundstrom, and the other, less experienced Swedes, Connors and McEnroe arrived in Göteborg only four days before the finals began. The event was held indoors on an extremely slow clay court, and the Americans' lack of preparation on the unfamiliar surface did them in. Both Connors and McEnroe lost their matches in straight sets, with Connors later receiving a heavy fine for verbally abusing the umpire during his match. Sweden won the event when McEnroe and Fleming suffered their first Davis Cup loss ever.

The Americans' misconduct throughout the 1984 event effectively ended Ashe's tenure as Davis Cup captain; the following year, Tom Gorman replaced him. Ashe has since maintained his involvement in championship tennis by working as a commentator for both the ABC and HBO television networks. He also serves as cochairman of the USTA Player Development Committee, working to promote junior tennis in the United States. (He cofounded this program in 1968 to help underprivileged youths receive the opportunity to play tennis; originally called the National Junior Tennis League, it merged with the USTA in 1984.)

Ashe's many contributions to the sport were formally recognized in 1985, when he was inducted into the Tennis Hall of Fame in Newport, Rhode Island. In the years since then, he has continued to look out for the players' interests and to represent the sport in a dignified manner. Just like during his days on the circuit, he still donates his time freely to tennis clinics and other events that allow youngsters the opportunity to play and learn about tennis. "Ashe remains the game's ambassador at-large, as well as its conscience," *World Tennis* reported in 1987.

Yet tennis does not define all of Ashe's daily activities. Most important of all, he leads a richly rewarding home life in New York City with his wife, Jeanne, and their daughter, Camera Elizabeth, who was born in 1987. He has always been someone who cannot sit still, however, and as a result he has remained involved in a wide range of causes and projects. He has joined the fight against heart disease, serving as campaign chairman of the American Heart

Ashe was officially inducted into the Tennis Hall of Fame in 1985 for having put together one of the most illustrious careers in modern tennis. He began by winning his first amateur title at age 12 and finished up by compiling a record of 818–260 on his way to winning 51 of the 304 open tournaments he entered.

Association in its attempt to educate the public on the subject, and supports a number of charities. According to Ashe, "There's always somebody who wants to use your name—and I understand this—because we are visible and our identity can help a cause. I'll do what I can."

In July 1989, Ashe was part of a group of black businessmen (led by Bertram Lee, the former finance cochairman for Jesse Jackson's 1988 presidential campaign) that attempted—unsuccessfully, as it turned out—to acquire the Denver Nuggets basketball team. The deal would have made the Nuggets the first black-owned professional sports team in nearly half a century.

On top of all this, Ashe has made his mark as a noted author and scholar. He has written a biweekly column for the *Washington Post* and articles for *Tennis* magazine; he has contributed to an instructional tennis book, *Mastering Your Tennis Strokes* (1976), and has produced one of his own, *Arthur Ashe's Tennis Clinic* (1981); and he has penned several autobiographies: *Advantage Ashe* (1967), *Arthur Ashe: Portrait in Motion* (1975), and *Off the Court* (1981). He has also received honorary doctorates from Dartmouth College, Le Moyne College, Princeton University, St. John's University, and Virginia Union University, thereby proving himself to be a man of letters in more ways than one.

Yet without a doubt, Ashe's greatest scholarly achievement has been the completion of *A Hard Road to Glory*, a three-volume history of the black American athlete. When Florida Memorial College asked him in 1983 to teach a course entitled "The Black Athlete in Contemporary Society," he discovered during his preparations for the class that very little had been written on the topic. He resolved to remedy the situation, and five years later his massive, groundbreaking study of black Americans in sports was published. This widely praised work has since earned him a reputation as an expert on the subject and has led to many requests for him to lecture on the black athlete.

In addition, Ashe has written frequently about related issues for major newspapers and magazines around the country. Among other things, he is an outspoken critic of how universities make use of athletes, particularly black ones, to raise revenues for their schools yet show little interest in having them receive an education. "It's no secret that 75 percent of black football and basketball players fail to graduate from college," Ashe wrote to the *New York Times* in early 1989. "We should either get serious about academic standards or cut out the hypocrisy and pay college athletes as professionals." Well aware that schooling has helped to enrich his own life, he wants other athletes to enjoy a similar opportunity.

"It was pounded into me," Ashe explained to a group of students during a recent speech at Columbia University Law School, "that I must not only try harder, but be better." Clearly, he took this important lesson to heart while he was growing up and worked at it as intently as he practiced the rudiments of tennis. "The thing is," he has pointed out, "at any time, whoever is across the net, you are never really playing an opponent. You are playing yourself, your own highest standards, and when you reach your limits, that is the real joy."

Ashe's urgent appeal to get the most out of life took on greater impact when he announced to the world that he was suffering from acquired immune deficiency syndrome (AIDS). At an emotional news conference in midtown Manhattan on April 8, 1992, he revealed that he had contracted the life-threatening disease, apparently from a blood transfusion he received during a second heart-bypass operation in 1983. "Beginning with my admittance to New York

Hospital for brain surgery in September 1988, some of you heard that I had tested positive for HIV, the virus that causes AIDS," he told the press. "That is indeed the case."

Ashe underwent brain surgery after it was determined that a severe bacterial head infection was causing paralysis in his right arm. Subsequent medical tests revealed the presence of a parasitic infection, which in turn led to the discovery that he was infected with the human immunodeficiency virus (HIV). He kept this finding from the general public, however, for more than three years. "Any admission of HIV infection," he said at the 1992 news conference, "would have seriously, permanently, and—my wife and I believe—unnecessarily infringed upon our family's right to privacy."

In disclosing that he was suffering from AIDS, Ashe became the second major sports star within a matter of months to announce that he was infected with HIV. Earvin "Magic" Johnson, a three-time winner of the National Basketball Association's Most Valuable Player Award, retired from the professional ranks in November 1991 after learning he was HIV positive.

Unlike Johnson, Ashe chose to share his secret only with a close circle of family and friends, including Charlie Pasarell and Cliff Drysdale. "I knew even before Magic that if I wanted to go public I could possibly help," Ashe said about advancing the cause of AIDS awareness. "But I wasn't ready to go public with it because I had some things that I wanted to do, unfettered, so to speak. I knew that with the public still learning about AIDS, that would have been impossible, once you go public." He decided to reveal his condition only after a newspaper reporter called to ask if a rumor that the former tennis star was suffering from the disease was true.

"Certainly there could be no better spokesman for the cause," Drysdale told reporters, "because people can't point a finger and find anything negative with Arthur. There are no skeletons in his closet. And there is no more thoughtful an athlete."

Arthur Ashe, tennis champion, defender of human rights, and fighter against racism, died on February 6, 1993, in New York City. After lying in state in the governor's mansion in Richmond, Virginia, he was buried in his hometown following a funeral service in which he was praised not only for his achievements in the sport of tennis but also for his quiet dignity and unshaken beliefs. ❧

APPENDIX:
TOURNAMENT WINS AND DAVIS CUP
RECORD

Arthur Ashe played in hundreds of tournaments during his career. Listed below are only the top events that he won.

In addition to capturing these titles, he was a member of the U.S. Davis Cup team in 1963–70, 1975, 1977, and 1978 and served as captain of the squad from 1981 to 1984. The United States won the Davis Cup seven times while Ashe was a part of its team, in 1963, 1968–70, 1978, 1981, and 1982. His overall Davis Cup playing record was 27–5 in singles matches and 1–1 in doubles competition.

Year	Tournaments Won
1955	ATA 12-and-under singles; ATA 12-and-under doubles (with Willis Thomas)
1956	ATA 15-and-under doubles (with Willis Thomas)
1957	ATA 15-and-under singles
1958	ATA 15-and-under singles; ATA 15-and-under doubles (with Willis Thomas)
1960	ATA 18-and-under singles; ATA men's singles; U.S. Junior Indoors singles
1961	ATA men's singles; ATA men's doubles (with Ronald Charity); U.S. Junior Indoors singles; U.S. Interscholastics singles
1962	ATA men's singles
1963	ATA men's singles; U.S. Hardcourts singles
1965	NCAA singles; NCAA doubles (with Ian Crookenden)
1967	U.S. Clay Courts singles
1968	U.S. National singles; U.S. Open singles
1970	U.S. Indoors doubles (with Stan Smith); Australian Open singles
1971	French Open doubles (with Marty Riessen)
1975	WCT Championship singles; Wimbledon singles
1977	Australian Open doubles (with Tony Roche)

CHRONOLOGY

————— ❧ —————

1943   Born Arthur Robert Ashe, Jr., on July 10 in Richmond, Virginia

1947   Moves to Brook Field in Richmond

1949   Begins to play tennis

1953   Spends first of eight summers receiving tennis instruction from Dr. Robert Walter Johnson

1959   Ashe makes his debut at the U.S. National Championships

1960   Moves to St. Louis, Missouri, for senior year of high school, where he graduates with the highest grade point average in his class

1961   Wins an athletic scholarship to the University of California, Los Angeles (UCLA)

1963   Makes his debut at Wimbledon and as a member of the U.S. Davis Cup team

1964   Wins his first major grass-court title, the Eastern Grass Court Championships; receives the Johnston Award

1965   Wins the national collegiate singles and doubles titles

1966   Attends Arthur Ashe Day in Richmond; graduates from UCLA; inducted into the army; becomes assistant tennis coach at the U.S. Military Academy

1967   *Advantage Ashe* is published

1968   Wins the U.S. Nationals and U.S. Open men's singles titles; becomes America's top-ranked amateur tennis player; the United States wins the first of seven Davis Cups with Ashe as a member of the team

1969   Helps form the International Tennis Players Association

1970   Campaigns to have South Africa expelled from Davis Cup competition; acts as U.S. goodwill ambassador to Africa

1971   Discovers future tennis great Yannick Noah

1973   Helps organize a players' boycott of Wimbledon; makes first visit to South Africa

1975   Wins the WCT Championships and Wimbledon's men's singles title; becomes the top-ranked player in the world; *Arthur Ashe: Portrait in Motion* is published

1977   Marries Jeanne Marie Moutoussamy

1978   Wins last tournament of his career

1979   Suffers a heart attack; undergoes open-heart surgery

1980   Announces retirement as a tennis player

1981   Becomes captain of the U.S. Davis Cup team; *Off the Court* is published

1985   Inducted into the Tennis Hall of Fame

1988   *A Hard Road to Glory* is published

1992   Announces he is suffering from AIDS

1993   Dies of AIDS complications on February 6

FURTHER READING

Ashe, Arthur. *A Hard Road to Glory: A History of the African-American Athlete*. 3 vols. New York: Warner Books, 1988.

———. *Arthur Ashe's Tennis Clinic*. Norwalk, CT: Golf Digest/Tennis, 1981.

Ashe, Arthur, with Neil Amdur. *Off the Court*. New York: New American Library, 1981.

Ashe, Arthur, with Frank Deford. *Arthur Ashe: Portrait in Motion*. Boston: Houghton Mifflin, 1975.

Ashe, Arthur, and Clifford Gewecke, Jr. *Advantage Ashe*. New York: Coward-McCann, Inc., 1967.

Collins, Bud. *My Life with the Pros*. New York: Dutton, 1989.

Collins, Bud, and Zander Hollander, eds. *Bud Collins' Modern Encyclopedia of Tennis*. Garden City, NY: Doubleday, 1980.

Evans, Richard. *Open Tennis: The First Twenty Years*. London: Bloomsbury, 1988.

Little, Alan. *Wimbledon Men: A Hundred Championships, 1877–1986*. London: Wimbledon Lawn Tennis Museum, 1986.

McPhee, John. *Levels of the Game*. New York: Farrar, Straus & Giroux, 1969.

Robertson, Max. *Wimbledon, Centre Court of the Game*. 3rd ed. London: BBC Books, 1987.

Robinson, Louis, Jr. *Arthur Ashe: Tennis Champion*. Garden City, NY: Doubleday, 1967.

Trengove, Alan. *The Story of the Davis Cup*. London: Stanley Paul & Co., Ltd., 1985.

USLTA Official Encyclopedia of Tennis. New York: Harper & Row, 1972.

INDEX

PICTURE CREDITS

———————— ❦ ————————

TED WEISSBERG is a journalist whose profiles of prominent athletes have appeared in *Current Biography*. A graduate of Wesleyan College, he currently resides in New York City with his wife.

NATHAN IRVIN HUGGINS is W.E.B. Du Bois Professor of History and Director of the W.E.B. Du Bois Institute for Afro-American Research at Harvard University. He previously taught at Columbia University. Professor Huggins is the author of numerous books, including *Black Odyssey: The Afro-American Ordeal in Slavery, The Harlem Renaissance,* and *Slave and Citizen: The Life of Frederick Douglass.*